Speaking Spanish

Like a Native

Speaking Spanish

Like a Native

Brad Kim

Erika Domínguez

Copyright © 2005, Brad Kim, Erika Domínguez
ISBN-13: 978-0-9764518-0-8

Kim, Brad.
  Speaking Spanish like a native / by Brad Kim and
Erika Domínguez.
    p. cm.
  Includes index.
  English and Spanish.
  LCCN 2005924235
  ISBN-13: 978-0-9764518-0-8
  ISBN 0-9764518-0-8

  1. Spanish language—Conversation and phrase books.
2. Spanish language—Textbooks for foreign speakers—
English. 3. Spanish language—Self-instruction.
I. Domínguez, Erika. II. Title.

  PC4121.K47 2005   468.3'421
                        QBI05-200100

Copyedited by Vitalee Giammalvo
Design & layout by Val Sherer

This book is dedicated to my wife, Erika Lizette, and our baby girl, Natalia, who are my inspiration and the loves of my life. I also dedicate this book to you, the reader, because I share in your excitement to learn Spanish and hope that this book helps you to achieve that goal.

Contents

Acknowledgments

For Best Wife in a Supporting Role:

Erika for being there every step of the way. Okay, so you accidentally deleted my entire first draft. All is forgiven. I just hope you can forgive me for having to spend all of those nights alone while I was on the computer until two o'clock in the morning. *Mil gracias* not only for your steadfast emotional support but especially for your specific insights regarding phraseology of the Spanish language. This book could not have been brought to fruition without your invaluable contribution.

For Best Unedited Tongue in Mexico:

My mother-in-law—the incomparable straight shooter—Choco Díaz de Domínguez, who tells it like it is … uncut and uncensored. Her knowledge of the curse words and other less-refined manners of speaking provides the reader with a taste of authentic native conversation.

For Best Actors in an Epic Drama:

Though there was no acting involved, my wife and I deserve this distinction for surviving all of the apartment flooding, the ceiling caving onto the living room floor, car troubles, and other dramatic events, all of which delayed the completion of this book over a three-year span.

For Best Supporting Cast:

We expecially wish to acknowledge our beloved family and friends. A special thanks goes to Ofelia Dueñas for reading the manuscript and for sharing so many practical phrases that truly enhanced the quality of this book. I am also indebted to my father, Kieun, for believing in our project, and to Patricia and Seton Schiraga for their constructive input and critique. A standing ovation for Kiki Domínguez, who has been there for us unconditionally from day one. A shout out to my *compadres* and *comadres* from Guadalajara, Mexico City, Culiacán, Mazatlán, Ensenada, Los Angeles, and San Francisco—for verifying and confirming that the Spanish contained in this book is actually spoken in their neck of the woods.

The Lifetime Acheivement Honors go to:

My mother, Kathryn, who has been there for us every minute of every day. Thanks for your unwavering support through it all.

1

An Introduction to the Game

Fans vs. Players

You can't really call yourself a swimmer if you don't get wet. Likewise, your chances of becoming the next great running back are pretty slim if you enjoy the football game more while sipping Gatorade from the safety of the sidelines. If your only ambition is to watch the game, then you're a fan, which is perfectly fine. You can be the one cheering on your favorite players, buying their jerseys, and watching them celebrate each victory. If you want to play, however, then you're going to have to learn how to become a "player."

In the world of professional sports, the odds are stacked a mile high against you. If you want to become a player in the Spanish language, then your chances of success rest entirely in your hands. In order to get there, however, you will need to jump the stands and take the field. The field is where the game is won or lost. It is where one can hear what the players really say in the huddle—not the edited, cut-and-pasted versions we read in the newspaper the next day. The purpose of this book is to make you sweat a little, to loosen your tongue only to have you bite it later, to expose you to the thrill of victory while minimizing your agony of defeat. Most importantly, *Speaking Spanish Like a Native* is like a playbook drawn out for *you*. Learn it well and your appreciation and understanding of the game will increase dramatically.

So what sets this book apart from others? It's unique because it brings the field to *you*—freshly cut and trimmed, with much of the information you probably already knew from beginning Spanish already weeded out. You get a view of authentic communication with real people in natural, everyday situations with family and friends just as you would experience in your own native language. This book is replete with words, phrases, and expressions that I learned by staying up until the wee hours of the morning chatting with native speakers in Mexico, and by sharing ideas, drinking beer, playing cards, dancing, cracking jokes, and even fishing. It is a written recording of a real game and real "players" transcribed onto paper, and like a truly dedicated reporter covering a breaking story, I was there to record it all … straight from the mouths of Latino speakers.

Sure, you will certainly experience growing pains in your quest to learn Spanish, but one day, when that special moment arrives, it will be the Spanish language that will give birth to *you*—opening your eyes to a world that has always been there but just never in focus.

So ... We Meet Again

Things always happen when you least expect it. It seems like ages ago that I was first introduced to the Spanish language. I was at the bottom of the food chain as a freshman in high school. For four years I battled my way through eight semesters of Spanish until finally graduation arrived—the day I would never have to speak another word of this foreign language called Spanish ... or so I thought.

After high school I attended college in San Diego, just a hop, skip, and a jump from Mexico. Yet Mexico was as alien to me as Mars. I only visited Tijuana twice—each time to buy fireworks, a poncho, a piggy bank, and a *sombrero* on my way back across the border. *Enchilada, burrito, carne asada, quesadilla,* and *taco* were the only Spanish words I had spoken since high school, even after spending my entire college years a short step away from Mexico, one of the most beautiful cultural gold mines in the world.

After college destiny took the wheel, slammed on the accelerator, and put itself on a collision course right into my path. I was heading towards another encounter with the Spanish language, but I just didn't know it at the time. My first job had me packing my bags to go and live in Mazatlán, Mexico, where the company I worked for had formed a joint partnership with a local seafood-processing plant that exported shrimp and squid to the United States. I accepted the challenge of broadening my cultural horizon with an open mind. So, I packed my luggage and a large bagful of books in order to pass the time. During my entire stay in Mexico, I never opened the bag of books. Bored? Are you kidding? I was thrown into a foreign-language ocean with barely enough skills to doggy-paddle, but I had the time of my life trying. The funny thing is that my years of high school Spanish mysteriously oozed back into my memory after being dormant for so many years. Even so, trying to speak with native Spanish speakers was a lopsided affair, to say the least. They spoke a mile a minute and used so many colloquial and slang terms that my head started spinning around in a sea of words. I was a little-league batter up against major-league pitchers who were throwing nasty curveballs, whizzing fastballs, and tricky knuckleballs. I could only really hit the underhand slow-pitch, and even that was a struggle at times.

They say, in Rome, do as the Romans do, and that was my strategy for living in Mexico. I was determined to speak like a local. During my first week in Mexico I bought a new blue spiral-bound notebook and started writing down every single English word or phrase I desired to know. Then I would ask sympathetic native speakers around the office to help translate them into Spanish. I carried this notebook everywhere I went: to dinner, to the theater, to the market. I jotted down all new words and included anything of interest that I heard on Spanish television. Soon the notebook was filled up from cover to cover.

One event of colossal importance that further fueled my desire to learn Spanish was my falling in love with Erika, who is now my wife and the mother of our daughter, Natalia. Erika was born and raised in Mexico, so in the beginning, communication was practically limited to playing charades in order to get our ideas across. Learning to speak Spanish, however, would later prove to be the key into her world and allowed me to forge wonderful relationships with her entire network of family and friends.

Unfortunately, my work in Mexico ended one day, but my quest to learn Spanish hasn't diminished since. Upon my return back to the States, I continued with my notebooks and I unabashedly continued to carry them with me everywhere I went. Eight years later, there I was with a ton of information crammed onto the rumpled pages of four tattered notebooks plus about one hundred pounds of scrap paper. It's a miracle that the notebooks were even still intact. So now what was I to do with all of this information? Well, scared of accidentally losing all the information I had so diligently accumulated, I decided to consolidate it by alphabetically arranging it into my computer. Then it dawned on me: In spite of searching far and wide, I had never found the intermediate Spanish book I was seeking. Suddenly, I realized that I had already written the book I was looking for. It was unorganized and unpolished, but it was in my possession the entire time. Thus, *Speaking Spanish Like a Native* was born.

What does a book written by a Korean American actually mean? It means that you will learn from the perspective of an average Joe. It means you will hopefully appreciate my humble beginnings—how I went scratching, clawing, and sometimes kicking my way through Spanish, just as you, too, may be doing right now. While Spanish comes more naturally to native speakers who are immersed in it, my growth spurt in Spanish occurred only after I put in all too many years of stumbling in frustration and confusion. You and I are probably not all that different. I believe that you, the reader, are much more connected to this book than you probably imagine. I can guarantee that I had the same questions you had and made the same mistakes you are likely making today. With this in mind, I didn't take the subtleties and common pitfalls of the language for granted. Instead, I took all of them into consideration while writing this book.

In the ensuing pages, I share with you everything I learned from the locals in Mexico, from native Spanish speakers here in the United States, from Spanish-language television and radio, and from everything I learned just by being curious enough to ask. I hope you find this book a valuable resource that will allow you to carry on a conversation more skillfully and confidently with native speakers, in their terms.

Keeping It Real

All people have different tastes. When you offer your guests a beverage, some just desire a simple glass of water. Others prefer an exotic, flavorful drink. Likewise, when it comes to language learning, some speakers are more colorful; they spice up their conversation with their own flavors and unique tastes. This means they all develop their own way of speaking. Their accents, vocabulary, slang, idioms, and sometimes even grammar have their own swagger from region to region, and are still evolving as we speak. At its core, however, it's still Spanish.

Having said that, you should realize that this book cannot be all things to all people. It leans towards Spanish spoken in the Americas, with one foot firmly planted in Mexico. The good news is that if you're going to pick a flavor, you have certainly picked a good one. At least here in the United States, Spanish as spoken in Mexico pulls a lot of weight because of Mexico's huge cultural influence and the fact that we are blessed with such a diverse Mexican population. Furthermore, you will realize that for this very reason, Spanish speakers who come from other countries and reside in the United States do understand (at least to some degree) the Mexican flavor of speaking.

Lastly, I must reassure you that *Speaking Spanish Like a Native* does not neglect the more elementary expressions. A great percentage of the examples in this book are in fact universal, and for those that are not, you will often be presented with other options for expressing the same thoughts. In the end, Spanish is still Spanish, no matter where you are. As a student of the language, you must take in whatever you can, even if only one drop at a time, because in Spanish there are no words that can be thrown away; they can only be recycled. Therefore, store these words in your mind's closet but leave the door open.

2

Do-It-Yourself Spanish

Learning any language will always be a do-it-yourself process, and I can tell you with one hundred percent certainty that you will get out of it what you put into it. As you browse through the Spanish-language section of any bookstore, you will encounter many useful books that might catch your eye with titles claiming you will be speaking Spanish in a day or week. Though their claims may be technically true, exactly how much Spanish you will be speaking and how much you want to speak are the questions you have to ask yourself. Every book will teach you something valuable but none can teach you everything you need and want to know, so don't expect this wonderful journey of learning Spanish to be a quick trip to the candy store. If done right, your language learning will be a marathon and not a sprint. Learning Spanish will require stamina, conditioning, and focus, and I assure you it won't be a ten-second dash to the finish line. Here's a list of tools you will need to get through it all.

Getting Started

Before you get started you will need the following:

- A hammer to hit the nail on the head

- Extra screws in case yours come loose

- Fully charged batteries (not included)

- A measuring tape to keep track of your progress

- Glue to hold yourself together

- A wrench to get a grip on mystifying grammatical structures that may drive you nuts

- A screwdriver or other beverage of choice to celebrate your little successes and achievements along the way

- Most importantly, you will need guts and determination to quell whatever inhibitions and fears you have

Instructions

1. Seeing is believing

Visualize your ultimate goal and purpose for learning Spanish. Picture yourself speaking fluently at home, at work, or on vacation in a Spanish-speaking country; or picture yourself being able to court your Spanish-speaking love interest. Whatever your motivation may be, picture it and frame it.

2. Mind over matter

Open this book when you're ready to read, but open your mind when you're ready to learn. You're probably used to doing things *your* way. When you learn a foreign language, however, you'd better get used to doing things *their* way. You're not going to reinvent the language. Believe me, I have already tried.

3. Speak now or forever hold your peace

Sure, you have the right to remain silent but when learning a language, taking the Fifth is not going to do you any good. Understandably, you may lack the confidence to speak or you may be a little shy, but how far you want to progress is entirely up to you, and it starts with opening your mouth.

4. Monkey see, monkey do

Watch Spanish-language television or talk with Spanish speakers whenever you can so that you develop a feel for how words are pronounced and in what context they are used. You can read in a book that horses say, "Neigh," but you'll never recognize the sound of a horse in real life unless you actually hear it from the horse's mouth.

5. Show me the money

When you learned to ride a bike, how many times did you fall or crash into your neighbor's car before you started popping wheelies? When you learned how to swim, how many times did you run out of energy and have to swim to the edge of the pool for a breather before you started doing continuous laps? Nobody said it was going to be easy, but by learning Spanish, you can reap a huge return if you invest enough time and energy.

Troubleshooting

Problem: You say, "tuh-*MAY*-toe," and I say, "tuh-*MAH*-toe."

Solution: English, as spoken in the United States, is somewhat flexible when it comes to pronunciation, and this flexibility is widely accepted. New Yorkers, Bostonians, Texans, and Californians, for example, can all have distinctly different pronunciations for the same words. Thus, you can say, "tuh-*MAY*-toe" and I can say, "tuh-*MAH*-toe." In Spanish, however, each letter of every word is supposed to be pronounced the same way, all the time. Thus, *tomate* (tomato) should always be pronounced "toh-mah-teh." Pronunciation is a key factor in becoming (or at least sounding) fluent, and perception is reality. If you sound fluent, you've already established some degree of credibility. The better you nail the accent down, the more efficiently and effectively you will master the language.

Problem: You say, "restroom," and I say, "bathroom."

Solution: Like in English, almost everything in the Spanish language can be expressed in more than one way, so don't just learn one word and shut the door on the synonyms. Otherwise, you may know the word *piscina* (swimming pool) like the back of your hand but have no clue what someone is saying when he or she asks you to go to the *alberca* (another word for swimming pool). To make matters more complicated, it is important to note that different countries (and even different regions within the same country) often use the same word differently. Take the word *camión,* for example. In Mexico, this word is generally understood to mean "bus." In many other Latin American countries, however, it means "truck." This may appear to be only a minor difference, but should you use the word *camión* to ask where the bus stops to someone who understands this word to mean "truck," you could find yourself stranded for quite some time.

Problem: I'm confused by all the changes in verb conjugations, pronunciation, formal versus informal, and masculine and feminine forms. To me, it's all mumbo jumbo.

Solution: If the ABCs of Spanish grammar are what you need, then maybe you should consider making this the *second* Spanish book you read. *Speaking Spanish Like a Native* assumes some prior knowledge of all these areas. Go back and review as needed.

Problem: I feel overwhelmed with all the information and can't seem to take it all in.

Solution: Rome wasn't built in a day. This book wasn't written in a day, and you won't understand everything in this book in a day. This is not a computer program that can be downloaded into your mind with the click of a button. Relax and take your time.

Problem: I've never heard of many of the words and phrases in this book and for those I am familiar with, I know a much easier way to say the same thing.

Solution: That's great because you need to know them all, but this book purposely omits many of the basic words you may already know. *Speaking Spanish Like a Native* contains words that a native speaker uses, and it's meant for those who want to be able to *blend* into a conversation, not stick out.

Problem: That's not how we say it in English.

Solution: Thinking that *everything* in English should literally translate into equal words in Spanish is a common mistake (See item 2 under "Instructions"). For a good example of this, see "Ton" in chapter 5.

Problem: A lot of the words and phrases contained in this book are not in the dictionary.

Solution: That's why they're in this book. A dictionary is a dictionary and that's all it is. It is not divine scripture. The fact that a word or phrase may not be in a dictionary does not mean that it doesn't exist. In the same way, if a particular store is not listed in the Yellow Pages, does that mean the store doesn't exist? If you study Spanish as spoken by native speakers, you won't hear them speaking strictly according to the principles outlined in any Spanish grammar or vocabulary book. Like any language, after the basics the language sort of runs on its own and evolves. The words and phrases contained in this book are all valid and in wide circulation.

Problem: The definitions of many of the words and phrases in this book are totally different from those given in the dictionary.

Solution: Don't panic. That's the difference between writing and speaking. We simply use spoken words more loosely and creatively, and there is less fear of being misunderstood because we can always clarify ourselves by using other terms. Dictionaries do not provide the same luxury.

General Housekeeping Rules

Rule #1

This book is *not* a dictionary, and the fact that it is arranged alphabetically does not make it one. A dictionary is a hugely invaluable resource, but you'll never look up ninety percent of the words contained in it. On the other hand, almost everything in this book is immediately accessible and intended to be directly applied to real-life conversations in Spanish. With this in mind, I urge you not to read this book on a need-to-know basis similar to the sporadic and random manner in which we look things up in a dictionary. Instead, read this book from cover to cover. By doing so, you will see that there is a logical cohesiveness to this book and to Spanish conversation itself. Fiddle around with the many phrases and try to make them your own by applying them in the context of your own life, since we tend to remember things better when we can make them personally meaningful.

Rule #2

Throughout this book you will see adjectives and nouns in Spanish followed by the letter "a" in parentheses. This means the word has a masculine and a feminine form depending on whether the person addressed or speaking is male or female. As you probably already know, "o" generally denotes a male, whereas "a" generally denotes a female. Common practice has always put the masculine form first. Some dictionaries only give the masculine form although modern day women and men may not agree with this practice. Let's take a look at a few examples. The adjective *tacaño(a)* means "cheap." If it takes three people to pull the dollar bill from Carlos's tight fist, then he can be described as *tacaño*. Likewise, a cheap (tightfisted) female could be called *tacaña*. Now take the word *coqueto(a)* (flirt). *Coqueto* with an "o" at the end is masculine, so your womanizing friend, Marcos, falls in this category. If it's Martha who bats her eyelashes and shows too much skin to the men, then change the "o" ending to the feminine "a" for *coqueta*.

Rule #3

Some words, especially adjectives that end in "e," are not gender specific. That is, the ending is constant and does not change regardless if you are speaking about a male or female. These words do not distinguish gender and will not be followed by the "a." The word *valiente* (brave) is one such example. *Él es valiente* is how one would say, "He is brave," and *Ella es valiente* means "She is brave."

Rule #4

In informal Spanish conversation, there are countless words that are used as both adjectives and nouns. This is not so often the case in English, though we might say, "You silly" instead of "You silly kid." Here, the word "silly" is actually used as a noun, although grammatically speaking it is not a complete sentence. The reality, of course, is that we simply speak much more informally (and even grammatically incorrectly) than we write. In Spanish, *enfadoso* (annoying) is an adjective, but you will often hear it used as a noun in conversation. *Este enfadoso no me dejaba en paz* = This annoying guy wouldn't leave me alone. How do I know it's an annoying guy? I know it because the ending is masculine (see Rule #2).

In other instances, however, certain words are in fact grammatically correct as either part of speech. The word *mandón(a)* is one such example. This word is an adjective meaning "bossy," but it is also used correctly as a noun meaning "bossy person" depending on the context in which it is used.

Throughout this section, you will encounter many Spanish words that are used as either adjectives or nouns in conversation. Since, however, this book focuses on real, informal conversation, I have decided to annotate the vocabulary contained in this section with the part of speech as commonly heard in informal conversation among native Spanish speakers. Therefore, if words are used as both adjectives and nouns in conversation, they will be noted as (adj. and n.).

To illustrate this explanation, I have provided several examples below:

Sangrón(a) (adj. and n.)

Example as an adjective:	*Ella es bien sangrona* = She's so stuck-up.
Example as a noun:	*La hermana de Pedro no me cae bien porque es una sangrona* = I don't like Pedro's sister because she's a stuck-up person.

Coqueto(a) (adj. and n.)

Example as an adjective:	*Mi hermano es muy coqueto* = My brother is very flirtatious.
Example as a noun:	*Este coqueto trató de agarrar mi mano* = This flirt tried to grab my hand.

Mandón(a) (adj. and n.)

Example as an adjective:	*¡No seas mandón!* = Don't be bossy!
Example as a noun:	*Mi primo es un mandón con todos sus hermanos* = My cousin is a bossy person with all of his brothers and sisters.

3

First & Last Impressions

All the Hellos and Good-byes You'll Need to Know

Comings and goings, introductions, salutations, farewells, and well wishes of the Spanish language are some of the most elementary yet important words you can learn. They are often the first things you say to someone and the last things you say before you part ways. In any language it is always proper protocol to be polite and make sure to greet people when you meet them and give them their due respect when you walk away. Even just a few kind words go a long way, and minding your manners will surely keep a friendly door open, should you meet again.

Now, before you pass this chapter off as a waste of your time, remember that even the best of us can mess up, and there's nothing more distracting and awkward (and sometimes hilarious) than replying to a greeting like this:

Greeting:	*¿Qué tal?* (How are you doing?, How's everything?)
Inappropriate reply:	*Nada mucho.* (Nothing a lot.)
Analysis:	The word *mucho* in Spanish means "many" or "a lot" but our first instinct may be to translate this to mean "much." By responding with *Nada mucho,* you are actually saying, "Nothing many" or "Nothing a lot." The words *nada* and *mucho* contradict each other, so you can imagine why native Spanish speakers find this incorrect reply to be quite humorous.

| Appropriate reply: | There are many correct responses you could give here, but perhaps the easiest and most common would be a simple *Bien gracias,* which means "Good, thanks" or "Fine, thanks." |

Greeting:	*¿Qué ondas?* (What's up?)
Inappropriate reply:	*Bien.* (Fine.)
Analysis:	Unlike *nada mucho* in the previous example, the word *bien* is a perfectly good response—but just not for this particular greeting. It is, however, quite a common blunder as far as greetings go. Watch out for this one.
Appropriate reply:	There is a list of good responses that fit nicely here, but the most typical reply seems to be the uninspiring *Nada* (Nothing).

The purpose of this chapter is to make sure you nail down your hellos and good-byes so that you come across as a socially competent, well-mannered person. This chapter will also help you to avoid embarrassing blunders by familiarizing you with many of the common greetings and good-byes you will encounter every day. Note: For the sake of simplifying the examples, everything is expressed in the singular informal *tú* form. In the real world, you will often be required to speak more formally, that is, in the more respectful *usted* form.

The Three B's

The Three B's (*Buenos días, Buenas tardes,* and *Buenas noches*) are the most common everyday greetings. That is, they are not specific to gender or age because there is no verb to conjugate, no masculine or feminine endings, no formal-versus-informal way of saying them, and generally speaking, the entire Spanish-speaking community uses the Three B's in the same manner. What separates these greetings from the rest is the fact that they are used both as greetings and good-byes. And wait … it gets better. You don't even have to think of a reply when one of the Three B's is said to you. Just repeat the same thing back. Someone says, *"Buenos días";* you just say, *"Buenos días"* right back. It's that easy. The only thing to keep in mind is that these expressions are time-specific and should be spoken within their allotted time slots, so keep an eye on your watch until you get the hang of it.

Buenos días	**Good morning**
	Buenos días is like our coffee as far as greetings go, because these are the words we wake up to each morning, but rarely is the coffee ever served black. People like this greeting with a lot of cream and sugar, so when you say it, mean it. Put some expression and enthusiasm into your voice. There is no written rule that I know of that specifies exactly what time of day the Three B's are spoken; however, the general consensus among native speakers is that this distinction is determined more by what the clock says rather than by how sunny or dark it is outside. Understandably, it may feel awkward to say, *"Buenos días"* at one o'clock in the morning when it's still pitch dark outside, but this greeting is said from 12:00 AM until 11:59 AM.

Buenas tardes   **Good afternoon**

Hopefully, by the time noon rolls around, your good morning has become a good afternoon. Regardless, from 12:00 PM to 5:59 PM, it is now *buenas tardes* instead of *buenos días.*

Buenas noches   **Good evening**

By now perhaps the hustle and bustle of the afternoon is winding down. Whether or not it is still light outside, it is now *buenas noches,* from 6:00 PM until 11:59 PM. *Buenas noches* is the "nightcap," meaning "Good evening" as well as "Good night" (before retiring to bed).

Absentee Formalities

There will be plenty of occasions when you want to say hello or good-bye to someone who is not present. In such cases, you have someone else do the task for you (you'll see what I mean in the examples below). In Spanish, these situations call on the use of *despedirse* (to say good-bye) and *saludar* (to say hello, to give your regards). They are what I call "absentee formalities," because you're having someone else say them on your behalf.

Saludar = To say hello
Mandar saludos = To send regards, Say hello to

Usually these verbs work as a tag team. Let's suppose Rosa is talking on the phone with her cousin Chabela in Mexico, but Rosa's husband, Davíd, doesn't have time to get on the phone to say hello. He might tell his wife, Rosa, "*Salúdamela*" (Say hello to her for me). On his behalf, Rosa will then relay the message as "*Te manda saludos Davíd*" (Davíd sends you his regards). If Davíd wanted to send his regards to Chabela's entire family, then he would tell Rosa, "*Salúdamelos*" (Say hello to them for me). Then, of course, Rosa would appropriately say, "*Les manda saludos Davíd.*"

Despedirse = To say good-bye (literally: to take leave of)

You're on vacation visiting your friends in Mexico. Tomorrow you're heading back to San Francisco, so at your going-away party, you say good-bye to everyone except Luis, who was unable to make it to the gathering. So, you tell Octavio (who *was* at the party) to say good-bye to Luis on your behalf, by saying, "*Despídeme de él*" (Tell him good-bye for me). If several friends were unable to attend the get-together, then you tell Octavio, "*Despídeme de ellos*" (Say good-bye to them for me).

Greeting's Greatest Hits

The greetings contained in this section are the classic everyday greetings that will never go out of style. You will already recognize all or most of them. Many of them mean the exact same thing in different words. Become familiar with these variations and have a response ready for each phrase or else you may offend a person if you just stare blankly after you have been greeted.

¿Cómo estamos?	**How are we?**

¿Cómo estamos? (How are we?) is a good choice of greeting when entering a room with more than one person. It is the general "umbrella" greeting covering everyone in the room so no need to give individual hellos.

¿Cómo estás?	**How are you?**

This is your standard, no-frills greeting and the workhorse of the group. Arguably, it is the most common of all the greetings.

¿Cómo has estado?	**How have you been?**

Haven't seen someone for a little while? Try this one.

¿Cómo te fue?	**How did it go?**

Use this greeting when you're curious to know how things went at your friend's audition, baseball game, party, piano lesson, school, office, dentist appointment, etc. Depending on the context in which it is spoken, *¿Cómo te fue?* is also a good translation for "How was it?" or "How did you do?"

¿Cómo te ha ido?	**How has everything been going for you?** **How has it been going?**

Say this when you haven't seen someone for a while and you want to know what's been going on since the last time you saw the person.

¿Cómo te va?	**How's it going?** **How are you doing?**

Just as frequently as you say, "How's it going?" in English, don't be shy to say this equivalent in Spanish.

Hola	**Hi, Hello**

It just doesn't get any simpler than *hola*. If you don't know this one already, where have you been?

¿No hay novedades?	**Nothing new?**

This is a casual and informal phrase one would say when having lunch with a friend one hasn't seen in a while.

¿Qué dices?	**What do you say?** **What are you saying?**

Probably a bit less frequently heard than some of the others but a worthy greeting to put into practice, nonetheless. Say this to your neighbor when you first see her in the morning, for example. However, *¿Qué dices?* is not always used as a greeting; when you don't understand what someone is saying to you, then *¿Qué dices?* also means "What are you saying?"

¿Qué haces?

What are you doing?
What are you up to?

This is not really a true greeting but more like a nonchalant half-greeting. You step into your friend's house and he looks occupied with something. Instead of saying, "*¿Cómo estás?*" ("How are you?"), you might choose "*¿Qué haces?*"

¿Qué hay?

What's new?

Actually, the correct greeting is *¿Qué hay de nuevo?* but it is often shortened to *¿Qué hay?* You'll be understood either way.

¿Qué hubo?

What's going on?

Grammatically speaking, *¿Qué hubo?* is a past tense construction. In conversation, however, it is understood as a present-tense expression similar to our "What's going on?" or "What's up?" Keep in mind that although not really correct, in some circles the pronunciation of this greeting has evolved to sound like *Kyoo-boh,* much the same as we say, "Wussup?" instead of "What's up?"

¿Qué ondas?

What's up?
What's the buzz?
What's shaking?

The hippest of all the greetings. You can't just say this to anyone, though. Keep it among your close circle or within the younger crowd. Don't be confused if you hear *¿Qué hongos?* It's just a made-up spin-off of *¿Qué ondas?*

¿Qué pasa?

¿Qué pasó?

What's happening?

¿Qué pasa? and *¿Qué pasó?* are conjugated in two different verb tenses, but in conversation both are interpreted in the present tense to mean "What's happening?" They are standard greetings that I'm sure you've already put to good use. Once in a while you might hear *¿Qué pasión?* which is youthspeak for *¿Qué pasa?*

¿Qué tal?

How are you?
How's everything?

This one is tricky because the natural tendency here is to think that *¿Qué tal?* is translated as "What's up?" "What's happening?" or any other greeting beginning with "what" (since *qué* means "what"). Actually, for some reason, the translation of *¿Qué tal?* is closer to "How are you?" or "How's everything?"

Good-bye's Greatest Hits

Now that you have gone through the greetings, naturally the next step is to learn the good-byes. You should never walk away from a friendly conversation without saying one of them. Leaving without saying good-bye will come across as unfriendly and discourteous as would arriving without saying hello. Here is the menu of farewells.

Abusado, Cuidado	**Be careful**
	Look out
	Watch out
	Someone from Mexico will understand you if you say, "*Abusado,*" but I can't guarantee the same about someone from another Spanish-speaking country. *Abusado* means "Be careful" or "Watch out." You say this to someone before he or she gets into a car for a long drive back home or to someone who has to walk home alone late one night, but not to your next-door neighbor who is going right home. If you want to play it safe, then say, "*Cuidado,*" which is universally understood.
Adiós	**Good-bye**
	Adiós should have been one of the first five words in Spanish you have ever learned.
Estamos en contacto	**We'll be in touch**
	You don't have to mean it to say it. In English we say it all the time and then often not contact the person for another year. What I'm trying to say here is that it's just another parting formality (not a promise), so don't think twice about using it.

Hasta la próxima   **Until next time**

It's kind of like our "Until we meet again" or "See you next time." This is less frequently used than some of the other expressions, but as I've been saying, you've got to vary your words a little every now and then.

Hasta luego   **Until later**
                          See you (later)

This is a simple, noncommitted, ambiguous farewell that can often be interpreted as "See you when I see you" because sometimes you don't really have any idea when you'll see the person again.

Hasta mañana   **Until tomorrow**
                          See you tomorrow

Although you can, you do not usually say, "*Hasta mañana*" to someone unless you actually believe that you might see that person the next day.

Nos vemos   **See you**
                          We'll see each other

Like *hasta luego*, *nos vemos* is a noncommitted, sometimes purposely ambiguous farewell, but that doesn't mean that it's a bad thing. It just means you don't have to feel guilty if you don't see each other anytime soon.

Que te vaya bien   **Take care (as you go on your way)**

If you're staying and someone else is leaving, then you can wish him or her well with *Que te vaya bien* (*Que les vaya bien* is the plural form). If you're leaving and the other person is staying, then don't say this phrase. Instead, the one who is staying will say it to you.

Que tengas

> ### Que tengas un buen día = Have a nice day
> ### Que tengas una buena tarde = Have a nice afternoon
> ### Que tengas una buena noche = Have a nice night

> Expressions with *que tengas* are some of the more cordial and pleasant leavetakings you can choose because you're not saying, "Good-bye," but rather you're wishing the person well on his or her way and in fact telling the person to have a good day, afternoon, or night.

4

Who's Who

Names, Nicknames, and *Niños*

Have you ever met someone named Francisco, whose buddies call him Pancho, or someone named Ignacio, whose family calls him Nacho? Don't be alarmed because you probably weren't calling them by the wrong names. They will respond to either—the latter being their nicknames (*apodos*). You may have also noticed that quite often many Latino children have the same names as their parents. Most of the time, the children are distinguished simply by adding the suffix "ito" or "cito" (for a male) and "ita" or "cita" (for a female) after the name or nickname. These suffixes mean "little" and they are similar to how we say "junior" in English. These endings are also used endearingly to mean "my little." For example, the elder Laura may call her daughter Laurita (Little Laura or My little Laura); Sergio—Sergito (Little Sergio or My little Sergio); Andrés—Andrecito (Little Andrés or My little Andrés); and so on. Not everybody has a nickname, but the brief sampling to follow will help you clarify who's who for those that do.

It is important to note that native speakers of Spanish also tack on these endearing suffixes to nonhuman types of adjectives and nouns. If you listen in on conversations between native speakers, you will hear these suffixes all the time. They are that common. For example, don't be surprised if someone offers you a *cafecito* (a little coffee) instead of *café* (coffee), or *lechecita* (a little milk) instead of *leche* (milk), perhaps with a *pedacito de pastel* (little slice of cake). You might even be advised to take your time while eating your cake and drinking your milk *despacito* (instead of *despacio*, which means "slowly").

The third column of the following list gives the diminutive forms, which can refer to children or express endearment. Note that even adults can be referred to with the diminutive forms.

Name	**Nickname**	**Niño**
Alberto	*Beto*	*Betito*
Consuelo	*Chelo*	*Chelito*
Enrique	*Kiki*	*Kikito*
Feliciano(a)	*Chano(a)*	*Chanito(a)*
Francisco	*Pancho*	*Panchito*
Gregorio(a)	*Goyo(a)*	*Goyito(a)*
Guadalupe	*Lupe*	*Lupita*
Guillermo	*Memo*	*Memito*
Ignacio	*Nacho*	*Nachito*
Isabela	*Chabela*	*Chabelita*
Jesús	*Chuy*	*Jesusito, Chuyito*
José	*Pepe*	*Pepito*
Luciano(a)	*Chano(a)*	*Chanito(a)*
Ramón	*Monchi*	*Monchito*
Roberto	*Beto*	*Betito*
Rosalío(a)	*Chalío(a)*	*Rosalito(a)*
Rosario	*Chayo*	*Chayito*

Who's Who in the Imaginary World

Just for fun, you might be curious to know who's who among some of our imaginary heroes, playpals, and animated TV stars. Movies have been made about some of the listed characters, and these characters have become universal in many Spanish-speaking countries. For example, the Hulk was once *El Hombre Verde* (The Green Man), but after the major motion picture was made, everyone now knows the name *El Hulk*. Before these movies, however, these characters had their own unique names translated into Spanish. Here is a short list of character names translated into Spanish as you would hear them in Mexico:

Barney Rubble	*Pablo Mármol*
Casper the Friendly Ghost	*Gasparín*
Cinderella	*La Cenicienta*
Daffy Duck	*Pato Lucas*
Donald Duck	*Pato Donald*
Fred Flintstone	*Pedro Picapiedra*
Green Lantern	*Linterna Verde*
Ninja Turtles	*Las Tortugas Ninja*
Popeye	*Popeye* (pronounced *poh-peh-yeh*)
Roadrunner	*Corre Caminos*
Smurf	*Pitufo*
Snow White and the Seven Dwarfs	*Blanca Nieve y Los Siete Enanos*
Speedy Gonzales	*Speedy Gonzales*
Spiderman	*Hombre Araña*
Strawberry Shortcake	*Rosita Fresita*
The Hulk	*El Hombre Verde*
Tweety Bird & Sylvester	*Piolín y Silvestre*
Wonder Woman	*Mujer Maravilla*
Woody Woodpecker	*El Pájaro Loco*

5

Talking the Talk
Means Walking the Walk

181 Steps Closer to Fluency

Talking the Talk Means Walking the Walk: 181 Steps Closer to Fluency is a collection of one hundred and eighty-one practical conversation boosters that will help you to advance and enliven your Spanish-speaking skills. Arranged alphabetically by the catchphrases or catchwords in English, this chapter will, in a sense, introduce you to the native speaker. It is a snapshot of words, phrases, and expressions taken from real conversations with native speakers. Dictionaries and grammar books are essential to learning any language and you will need to refer to them even while reading this chapter. You can't always, however, call a time-out in the middle of a conversation, pull out your dictionary, and look up a particular word or phrase. To keep a conversation flowing, you will need to know how to express yourself "conversationally," and this chapter will help you to accomplish that goal. These phrases are like your oil and your antifreeze—greasing the squeaky engine and keeping the motor running. Such words will help you to fill in the gaps, thereby keeping the conversation going when it gets cold. If you want to walk the walk of a native speaker, then you've got to talk the talk. *¡Buena suerte!*

Absorbed

Estar bien entrado(a) and *estar embebecido(a)* = To be "absorbed" or "fascinated by," "into," or "fixated on" something. You'll see examples of this during the World Cup when people are glued to the television set and not even a major earthquake can shake their attention away from the game. *Cuando papá está viendo el juego, está bien entrado* (or *embebecido*) *y no le hace caso a nadie* = When Dad is watching the game, he's totally absorbed (or "engrossed") and he doesn't pay attention to anyone. (This does not include being "into" or "fixated" on someone in whom you have a romantic interest. For that, see "Infatuated" later in this chapter.) Along the same lines, the verb *entrar* used in the negative can also describe someone who is just not mentally "into" some activity. By that I mean the party animal who was unusually quiet at the club or even the champion boxer who just didn't seem himself on fight night. *El boxeador perdió porque nunca entró de lleno a la pelea* = The boxer lost because he never fully got into the fight (maybe due to distractions or maybe because he wasn't really motivated).

Annoy

People annoying people—it's one of life's most assured guarantees. In Spanish, *enfadar, molestar, chocar,* and *fastidiar* all mean "to annoy." The indispensable "You're so annoying!" is *¡Qué enfadoso eres!* Although pestering your sister can be fun and is well within your job description as her sibling, you could occasionally exhibit a little compassion and tell your friends, *"Vamos a quedarnos callados porque no la quiero enfadar"* ("Let's keep quiet because I don't want to annoy her").

Appetite

The safe and predictable way to tell someone that he or she has a hearty appetite is by using the term *tener buen apetito*. Should you choose to venture beyond your safe and predictable ways, then *tener buen diente* is another option (literally meaning "to have a good tooth"). We might say this to a growing child who manages to finish everything on his or her plate or even to the guy who supersizes all his meals. *Tienes buen diente, te comiste toda la comida* = You have a good appetite; you finished all the food.

Arouse

To arouse someone's curiosity is *despertar la curiosidad*. *Lo que me dijiste de Víctor me despertó la curiosidad* = What you told me about Víctor aroused my curiosity. To arouse suspicion is *dar mala espina* (see "Make someone suspicious" in this chapter). To arouse someone sexually is *prender* or *encender* (see "Turn someone on" also in this chapter).

Back out, Flake out

Some people are just no good at honoring their commitments. It happens all the time, whether intentional or not, and that's why this phrase is an absolute must-know. *Rajarse* or *echarse para atrás* = To back out (flake out). *Hice un compromiso con mi amigo pero tuve que rajarme a la última hora* = I made plans with my friend but I had to back out at the last minute. *No te rajes* and *No te eches para atrás* both mean "Don't flake out" or "Don't back out." Just for your information, *echarse para atrás* also applies to backing one's car out of the garage, for example, but more typically it is said of someone who says he or she will do something or be somewhere but "backs out" in the end.

Backfire

The degree of difficulty in whipping this one out in conversation is about an 8.5 out of 10, but it's just that much more impressive should you stick the landing. *Salir el tiro por la culata* = To backfire. It is used to express how your plans, jokes, or tricks have worked against you or "backfired" on you. *Pedro pensaba que su plan era perfecto, pero al final le salió el tiro por la culata* = Pedro thought his plan was perfect, but in the end it backfired on him.

Bad influence

Sonsacar means to be a bad influence on someone by coaxing and enticing the person into doing something that is probably not in his or her best interest. Let's say your friend Arturo has a drinking problem. Saturday night rolls around and you and the entire gang suggest visiting the new bar down the street. Arturo's mother might warn everyone, "*¡No lo sonsaquen!*" ("Don't cajole him," or "Don't be a bad influence on him").

Beat around the bush

There are some people who just never get to the point, and their conversations sound like a never-ending string of words shooting off in every direction except the right one. I call it the "treadmill conversation" because it runs on and on without going anywhere. Whatever the reason, such individuals often need to be redirected at every intersection or they'll continue taking detours and never reach their final destinations. You can help them with the following expressions: *Andarse por las ramas* = To beat around the bush. *No te andes por las ramas* = Don't beat around the bush. *¡Ve al grano!* (Get to the point!) is another good phrase when you need to hear something straight. Here are a few more phrases that will help keep the conversation on track: *¿Qué tiene que ver eso?* = What does that have to do with it? *¿Qué caso tiene?* = What's the point? and finally, *Dime sin rodeos* = Tell me without going in circles.

Beg

Rogar = To beg. *No más te pedí un favor chiquito. No te voy a rogar* = I only asked you for a small favor. I'm not going to beg. For situations where more serious begging is required, use *pedir de rodillas* (to ask for on one's knees). After begging your wife to let you stay home to watch the football game instead of accompanying her to the tupperware party, you might finish the sentence by saying, "*Te lo pido de rodillas*" ("I beg you on my knees"). Saying this phrase, however, does not mean that you actually have to get down on your knees to beg unless you feel it might help your cause.

Bet

Apostar = To bet. *Te apuesto que te puedo ganar un juego de ajedrez* = I'll bet you that I can beat you in a game of chess. *Apostar* implies a more formal type of bet where something is usually on the line (money, a favor, a beer, or even just your pride), and the bet is usually sealed with a handshake or maybe just with your word.

There is also an informal expression for "bet" that translates more like "betcha." It is constructed with *"a que"* followed by whatever it is you're betting on. *A que Davíd no se presenta a la fiesta* = Betcha Davíd doesn't show up at the party. Here the usage of "bet" is meant usually as a passing comment but doesn't mean that you're willing to put your money where your mouth is. *"A que"* is also used to express the commonly used "betcha yes," "betcha not," betcha yes," "betcha not" in a kind of back and forth argument most of us surely had when we were kids. In Spanish it's *a que sí, a que no, a que sí, a que no.*

Blackmail

Chantajear = To blackmail. Your annoying little brother tells you, "If you don't give me that last piece of cake, I'll tell Mom you broke your curfew last night." There are obviously a million responses you could give, but for the purpose of this example, a fitting reply would be *"¡No me chantajees!"* for "Don't blackmail me!" I know, I know ... it's pretty difficult to pronounce. That's why you'll be happy to know that for most situations you can use the noun *chantaje* (blackmail) instead of having to conjugate the verb *chantajear*. So, the simpler and more general *"¡Puro chantaje!"* is all you have to say. It's like saying, "That's total blackmail!"

Blow someone's lid, Drive someone crazy

Sacar el tapón (literally, "to take the lid off") means "to make someone blow his or her lid" or "to drive someone crazy." It is said to express anger and frustration. You can use it when someone pushes you to the end of your patience. *Aloncito quiere a su hermana, pero ella le saca el tapón* = Aloncito loves his sister, but she drives him crazy.

Boo

More just for your information than for practical purposes: to "boo" someone is *abuchear*. This is not the kind of "boo" one might hear in a haunted house. It is the kind of "boo" you'll hear the home crowd give the visiting team when they're introduced before a game. The noun is *abucheo*. *Cuando presentaron el equipo visitante, los aficionados abuchearon muy fuerte* = When they introduced the visiting team, the fans booed loudly.

Brag

Presumir = To brag. Someone asks you, "Are you a good dancer?" You reply, *"No es que quiera presumir pero bailo muy bien"* ("I don't mean to brag but I dance really well"). *Tirar aceite* (literally, "to throw oil") also means to brag but is usually said about showing off or flaunting material possessions. *A Ana le gusta tirar mucho aceite, por eso compra pura ropa de moda* = Ana totally likes to flaunt it and that's why she buys only the latest fashions in clothing.

Brainwash

Lavarle el cerebro = To brainwash. Not to be confused with hypnotize (*hipnotizar*) or planting things in someone's head (*calentar la cabeza*), but it is almost a perfect cross between the two. *Mi amigo se metió en un culto y le lavaron el cerebro* = My friend got involved in a cult and they brainwashed him. In an effort to gain votes during an election year, politicians remind us of how sweet-sounding promises and a little charisma can go a long way. *Los políticos siempre le quieren lavar el cerebro al pueblo* = The politicians always want to brainwash the people.

Note: Sometimes you'll hear *cerebro* (brain) and *cabeza* (head) referred to as *coco* (coconut).

Broke

The verbs for breaking a vase or glass are *romper* or *quebrar*. *Andar quebrado(a)* and *andar tronado(a)*, however, are the verbs used to describe someone who is broke. *Mi vecino anda quebrado porque malgastó todo su dinero* = My neighbor is broke because he squandered all his money. *Ando muy tronado este mes porque Juan no me pagó lo que me debía* = I'm very broke this month because Juan didn't pay me what he owes me.

Bummed, Feeling down

Me siento mal (from *sentirse mal*) is the all-encompassing way to express "I'm feeling down," which also includes feeling depressed, sad, and sick. *Sentirse feo* works well, too. Though *feo* is typically associated with a physical ugliness, it is not always the case. It can also refer to the ugly manner in which your child talks back or the ugly manner in which the skateboarder fell off his board and smacked hard onto the asphalt, for example. In Mexico especially, you will also hear the verb *sentir gacho*, which means to feel "bummed" or "down" (but not sick). *Siento gacho porque salí mal en el examen* = I feel down because I didn't do well on the exam. *Sentí gacho porque mi mejor amiga, Marta, no me habló en mi cumpleaños* = I feel bummed because my best friend, Marta, didn't call me on my birthday. "What a bummer!" is *¡Qué gacho!* but in more formal company, you're better off with *¡Qué malo!*

Burp

The verb in Spanish is *eructar,* though you will often hear it as *eruptar* (spelled with a "p" instead of a "c"). You already know what a burp sounds like and have done it yourself a few thousand times. *Es mala educación eructar en la mesa* = It's impolite to burp at the table. This is generally true in Western cultures, but in some countries burping after a square meal is actually considered a polite stamp of approval, meaning that the food was to your satisfaction.

Butterflies in your stomach

To have butterflies in your stomach = *Tener cosquillas en el estómago.* Keep in mind, however, that the literal translation of "to have butterflies in your stomach" *(tener mariposas en el estómago)* has already caught on and may even be the better choice. Use this expression when *estar nervioso(a)* (to be nervous) doesn't quite explain that tingling, nervous sensation that feels like your stomach just dropped out from underneath you. You may get butterflies in your stomach before having to give a speech in front of a packed house, when on a roller coaster, or when that cutie you have a crush on enters the room. *Siento mariposas en el estómago cuando veo al muchacho que me gusta* = I get butterflies in my stomach when I see the guy that I like.

Catch someone off guard or by surprise

To catch someone off guard or by surprise can always be expressed with the general and straightforward *sorprender. Me sorprendiste cuando te oí hablar español* = You surprised me when I heard you speaking Spanish. One may also hear *agarrar de sorpresa* or *caer de sorpresa,* which mean exactly the same thing.

Agarrar en curva is a hip expression that also expresses being caught off guard usually in the act of doing something sneaky. For example, if you told your mom that you were going to church and she catches you walking into the movie theater, then you could tell her, *"Me agarraste en curva"* ("You caught me by surprise"). *Agarrar con las manos en la masa* (to catch someone with the hands in the dough) is another equally good expression for "to catch someone by surprise" or "in the act." Lastly, a simple *¡Te agarré!* (I caught you!) is a good choice for practical everyday usage. Say this when you catch someone doing something underhanded or even when you successfully pull a practical joke on someone.

Sacar de onda is another trendy expression worth knowing, but you must pay extra attention to the explanation in order to understand how to use it because it is slightly more complicated. *Sacar de onda* means to be caught off guard, to be surprised, to be "shaken up," or to be "beside oneself," but it is usually applied to situations where disappointment, shock, and disbelief are involved. Follow my examples. If on your twenty-first birthday you invited everyone to your party except for your closest friend, then your friend would have every right to tell you, *"Me sacaste de onda totalmente porque no me invitaste a la fiesta"* ("You totally surprised me because you didn't invite me to the party"). When someone accuses you of something bad that you obviously did not do, then tell the accuser, *"Me sacaste de onda porque me echaste la culpa por algo que no hice"* ("I'm beside myself because you blamed me for something that I didn't do"). For good measure, here's one more. You beat out thousands of contestants in the national singing competition only to barely miss the cut for the top five finalists and one million dollars in prize money. When a local reporter asks how you feel, you might say, *"Todavía estoy sacado(a) de onda"* ("I'm still shook up").

Catchy

Do you ever catch yourself singing or humming those cheesy jingles you hear on television commercials? As silly as you think they are, you remember them because *están pegajosos* (they're catchy) from the adjective *pegajoso(a)*, which also means sticky, in case you didn't know. Of course anything can be catchy—jingles, ideas, campaign slogans, people's names, and your favorite singer's new hit single. *Esa canción de Myriam* (a Mexican singer) *está bien pegajosa—siempre me agarro cantándola.* = That song by Myriam is very catchy—I always catch myself singing it.

Challenge

Desafiar or *Retar* = To challenge. *Te reto* and *Te desafío* both mean "I challenge you." *Te reto a ver quién termina la tarea primero* = I'll challenge you to see who can finish the homework first. Parents who find themselves reestablishing the rules, boundaries, or the hierarchy of authority in the house when their children challenge them will find good use for the verb *desafiar*. Suppose your fifteen-year-old daughter defiantly refuses to finish her homework and is intent on attending a college party in spite of your adamant opposition. You might be inclined to say, *"No me desafíes ... te estoy diciendo que no irás a la fiesta"* ("Don't challenge me ... I'm telling you that you're not going to the party").

Change the subject

Cambiar el tema is the universal way to say, "to change the subject." When you feel the need to get a little witty with your words, use *meter boruca* instead. It's the slang version of "to change the subject," but literally it means to cause distraction or an uproar in order to get the attention off oneself. Marco and his group of friends are reliving the most embarrassing moments of their lives. Finally, the focus of conversation comes around to Marco, and he is well aware that they are about to publicize the mortifying time he fell asleep in church and actually woke himself up from the sound and propulsion of his own fart (true story, by the way). So, in a desperate attempt to divert attention, he interrupts with, *"¿Pueden creer el clima tan malo que tenemos últimamente?"* ("Can you believe the terrible weather we've had lately?"). Your friends then shoot back with an accusing *"¡No metas boruca!"* ("Don't change the focus away from yourself!").

Chat

Hablar has always been the standard verb for "to talk," but we tend to get too comfortable in using it especially when another verb choice could be more appropriate. Though *hablar* is always correct, *platicar* is unequivocally the more precise translation for "to chat" or "to converse." *Me gusta platicar con mi tío Sergio porque siempre me cuenta historias chistosas* = I like to chat with my uncle Sergio because he always tells me funny stories.

There also exists another, less formal word for chat—*cotorrear*. *Cotorrear* means to chatter, ramble, or go on and on about something, but it doesn't necessarily mean that you're talking mere gibberish. *Siempre que veo a mis amigas nos gusta cotorrear por horas* = Every time I see my friends we like to ramble on for hours. To the girl in class who just won't stop talking, you could say, "*Ya para de hablar en la clase. ¡Eres una cotorra!*" ("Stop talking in class already. You're such a chatterbox!"). Note: *Una cotorra* is actually a parrot. The more formal and universally understood term for chatterbox is *platicador(a)*.

Cheat

To cheat in cards, final exams, or any type of test or competition that gives you the unfair advantage is *hacer chapuza, hacer trampa,* or *engañar. Esa cabeza hueca recibió buenas calificaciones sólo porque hizo chapuza en todos los exámenes* = That airhead got good grades only because he cheated on all the exams.

To cheat on somebody (infidelity) is expressed by the phrase *poner los cuernos* (literally, to "put the horns"). *Alicia rompió con su novio porque él le puso los cuernos* = Alicia broke up with her boyfriend because he cheated on her.

Check Out

To check out of a hotel is *checar de salida,* but this expression seems to be more familiar in Mexico than in other Latin American countries. *Chequear* is also commonly heard instead of *checar.* To check something out with no real meaningful purpose or specific agenda can be conveyed with the verb *bobear* or *abrir la boca.* You ask your brother why he's going to the mall and he responds, "*Nada más a bobear*" or "*Nada más a abrir la boca*" (literally, "just to open the mouth"). These expressions could mean anything from browsing and checking out the girls to just hanging out.

Zorrear is the verb for those specifically with wandering eyes (though you can also use *bobear*). It means to "check out" or "scam on" someone, and it's what some men and women do every time an attractive person walks by. *Mira a todos esos muchachos zorreando a las muchachas que entran a la tienda* = Look at all those guys checking out the women who are coming into the store.

Cheering up, Cheering on

Animarse is the word for "to cheer up." When someone is feeling down or depressed, then you can say, "*¡Anímate!*" for "Cheer up!" If you're sad because your brother left the country to work abroad, then someone could tell you, "*¡Anímate porque lo verás pronto!*" ("Cheer up because you'll see him soon").

Echar porras is how we cheer someone on (not up) as the home crowd would do for its team at a sporting event, for example. *Hay que ir a echarle porras a nuestro equipo en el torneo de baloncesto* = We should go to cheer on our team in the basketball tournament. Here's where things get more interesting. This can be a good sarcastic expression when one is being ganged up on. Suppose your mom put you in charge of mopping the kitchen floor while she ran errands. Upon her return, she questions if you completed your chore. Then your brother jumps in, saying, "Hey, I didn't see you mopping!" Then your sister joins in and says, "Weren't you watching TV the entire time?" If you find yourself in a similar situation, then you can tell your traitorous siblings, "*No vengan aquí a echarme porras.*" This is a purely sarcastic way of saying, "Oh, thanks for helping me out!" or "Thanks for coming to my rescue!" *Echar porras* is also quite a humorous expression to use on someone who is trying to make himself or herself feel better. Let's say, for example, that someone asks you what your astrological sign says about you. Skipping the part about your tendency to be stubborn, selfish, and hard to get along with, you respond, "It says I'm intelligent, creative, hardworking, and honest." At this moment one could jokingly interrupt with, "*¡Échate porras!*" which means "Cheer yourself up!" or a sarcastic "Whatever makes you feel better!"

Choke, Fold under pressure, Get stuck

Have you ever been totally prepared to nail down that all-important speech or to ask out that special someone only to stumble over your words and get tongue-tied when it came time to deliver? If so, then *se te atoró la carreta*. This means that you "choked" or folded under pressure (from the expression *atorarse la carreta*). In a less dramatic phrase, *atorarse la carreta* (or just *atorarse*) also means to "get stuck." For example, your boss may give you a difficult project to complete and then tell you, *"Háblame si se te atora la carreta"* or *"Háblame si te atoras."* (Both mean "Call me if you get stuck," but notice that the sentence construction differs with these two expressions. Pay attention to the verb endings.) If you get physically stuck, then you can use *atorarse* but not *atorarse la carreta*. *Se me atoró el pie entre las sillas* = My foot got stuck between the chairs.

Complain

It's one thing when someone just won't shut up. It's another thing when someone just won't cease to complain. Believe me, there are plenty of people who truly are unhappy unless they have something to complain about. "To complain" is *quejarse* and a complaint is *una queja*. *Ella no me cae bien porque siempre se está quejando de todo* = I don't like her very much because she's always complaining about everything. Perhaps the greater lesson to take from this is how to shut this person up. For that, skip ahead to "Shut someone up."

Copy

People are always copying other people, whether it be the signature moves of famous athletes, the fashion trends of the movie stars, the mannerisms of their older siblings, or even the test answers of the smartest guy in class. If imitation is the highest form of flattery, then I guess we should feel honored. In Spanish these acts of piracy are expressed with the verbs *arremedar* and *copiar* (to copy). *La hermana menor de Claudia siempre la arremeda* = Claudia's younger sister always copies her. *No me arremedes* and *No me copies* both mean "Don't copy me."

Cover for someone, Cover one's back

Before walking into enemy territory you might turn to your posse and say, "Cover me," "Watch my back," or "Get my back." In Spanish this is expressed by saying, *"Tápame"* (from the verb *tapar*) or *"Cúbreme"* (from the verb *cubrir*). If you want to express "covering up for someone," then also use *tapar*. *Luis siempre se sale con la suya porque su mamá siempre le tapa todo* = Luis always gets away with everything because his mother always covers up for him.

Cut in, Come between

Boy, do I love my dog and I'm glad he loves me, too, but what started out as a marriage between my wife and me quickly turned into a threesome with my dog, Morpheus, in the middle of everything. Guess who sleeps on the bed in between my wife and me every night? Guess who wedges between my wife and me while we're watching television on the sofa? I almost expect his puffy little head to pop out of the toilet when I lift the seat cover. To get to my point, I often complain, *"¡Siempre se cuela!"* which means "He's always cutting in!" or "He's always coming in between!" from the verb *colarse* (to cut in, slip through, slip in, or come between). *Colarse* is also used to explain how that jerk at the theater is cutting in line. *¡Mira como se cuela ese pendejo!* = Look how that jerk just cuts in line!

Cut one's losses (before things get worse)

Cortar por lo sano is definitely a phrase to remember, and if you don't often say it in conversation, it is a good phrase to live by. It means to stop things before they get worse, to cut one's losses and move on, and in a purely figurative sense "to quit while you're ahead." I say figuratively because it doesn't mean that anyone is necessarily ahead. This phrase is almost strictly used in situations involving people, so be careful not to use it when talking about cutting your losses on a failed business venture, for example. What started out as a "liar, liar, pants on fire" argument with your coworker Berta has gotten ugly. At this point one of you might decide to say, *"Más vale cortar por lo sano antes de que las cosas empeoren,"* which means "It's better to stop the bickering now before the bad feelings get worse." Let's say the argument between you and Berta got so ugly that it reached the point of no return. Then you could say, *"Terminé mi relación con Berta. Fue mejor cortar por lo sano porque ya teníamos muchos problemas*" ("I ended my relationship with Berta. It was better for me to cut my losses and move on because we already had many problems").

Cut someone down, Critique someone

Tijerear, for lack of a better definition, means to "cut through someone," "to cut someone down," or "to pick on a person," usually in a condescending manner. The person who does the "cutting" is called a *tijera,* which aptly means "scissors" in Spanish. Suppose you make a flattering comment about that elegantly dressed woman at the mall. The *tijera* would say, "Yeah, but her shoes are cheap. I saw them at a discount store." At a wedding you comment on how beautiful the bride looks. The *tijera* would say, "Yeah, but she's covering that big zit with her bangs." As you can tell, a *tijera* has an eye for flaws and imperfections. Though we're all *tijeras* in our own right, you won't be labeled one as long as you keep your comments to yourself.

Deal with, Put up with

There are a few different ways to express "dealing with" or "putting up with" people and situations. Familiarize yourself with each of these expressions so that you recognize them in conversation.

Poder lidiar con = To be able to deal with. *Delia no puede lidiar con los niños, son muy enfadosos* = Delia can't deal with the kids because they're very annoying. Even simpler, drop *lidear con* and just use the verb *poder* by itself. *Delia no puede con los niños* also means "Delia can't deal with the kids."

Aguantar is an equally good option. *Delia tiene que aguantar a Fernando porque es el novio de su hermana* = Delia has to put up with Fernando because he is her sister's boyfriend. When used as an exclamatory remark for "Deal with it!" your options are limited to *"¡Aguántate!"*

Now let's say that you can't "put up with" or "deal with" someone to the point where you can't stand the person. For that, use *soportar. Delia no soporta a su primo Oscar* = Delia can't stand her cousin *Oscar.* You could also say, *"Delia no lo soporta"* ("Delia can't stand him") if it's already understood that we're talking about her cousin Oscar.

Defend oneself

Defenderse = To defend oneself, but if you're more of a visual person, then you might consider the more graphic expression *sacar las uñas*. Like a cat, it means to "show your claws," but figuratively it means to be alert, to be on the lookout, or to be on the defensive and ready to fight if necessary. *No le puedo dar la contra a mi tía porque siempre saca las uñas* = I can't go against my aunt because she's always on the defensive and ready to shoot back. Note: *Defenderse* also means to "hold one's own," or "manage to get by" (see "Hold one's own" in this chapter).

Ditch

Sometimes you just need to get away, whether it be from that boring math class, that ruthless bully, or that annoying leech. In each case, the verb "to ditch" will help you do it. In the following examples, the verb "to ditch" is also commonly recognized as "to cut" or "to play hooky." In Spanish there are many different ways to indicate this concept. To ditch work is *faltar al trabajo*. *Falté al trabajo porque tenía cruda* = I ditched work because I had a hangover. To ditch or skip school is *irse de pinta*. "How was school today?" *No sé, me fui de pinta* ("I don't know, I ditched"). Now let's say you just can't get rid of that annoying leech who has declared himself your new best friend. Here, you call on the verb *deshacerse de* (literally, "to undo oneself from" or "to get away from"). *¿Cómo puedo deshacerme de Erik? ¡Es muy enfadoso!* = How can I get away from Erik? He's so annoying! To ditch, in the sense of avoiding someone by turning away before he or she sees you, is expressed with *sacar la vuelta*. So the next time you see annoying Erik coming your way, you might think, *"Le voy a sacar la vuelta antes de que me vea."* ("I'm going to turn away before he sees me.")

Do a favor

To "do a favor" in English is translated literally in Spanish as *hacer un favor*, but you should do yourself a favor and learn that *hacer un paro* also means the same thing except that it is used more among the younger, hipper generation. *Hazme el paro de ayudarme con el papeleo* = Do me the favor of helping me with the paperwork. Just be careful not to confuse *un paro* (a favor) with *puro paro* (pure lies).

Do a good job, Do a bad job

Hacer buen papel = "To do a good job" or "to do well." It can apply to almost anything, from singing well at the local karaoke contest to acing your midterm exams. *Estudié tanto porque necesitaba hacer buen papel en el examen* = I studied so much because I needed to do well on the exam. In the opposite respect, *hacer mal papel* means to do poorly. *Juan hizo mal papel en su trabajo anterior y por eso no lo contrató la compañía del Sr. Juárez* = Juan did poorly in his previous job and that's why Mr. Juárez's company didn't hire him. Keep in mind that *hacer buen/mal papel* also can mean to "make a good/bad impression." *Quiero hacer buen papel en la entrevista de trabajo* = I want to make a good impression at the job interview. Before meeting your girlfriend's parents for the first time, you might say to her, *"Quiero hacer buen papel cuando me presentes a tus padres"* ("I want to make a good impression when you introduce me to your parents").

Do as one damn well pleases

There are some people who just can't be told what to do, and any attempt to do so would prove to be a waste of time. They've already got their minds made up and their agendas set. These free-spirited individuals do what they damn well please. *Hacer su santa voluntad* is how we say it in Spanish. *Mi amigo Diego nunca me escucha y siempre hace su santa voluntad* = My friend Diego never listens to me and always does whatever he damn well pleases.

Do one's best

Sometimes it's all we can ask for. *Echarle ganas* = To do one's best or to try one's hardest. It is much like *hacer buen papel* (to do a good job), but these two expressions differ in one subtle aspect: *Echarle ganas* is used more as encouragement for someone to try his or her best, whereas *hacer buen papel* implies a stronger determination and need to succeed. Kids will often hear parents tell them, *"¡Échale ganas!"* to encourage them to put forth their best effort or to put their hearts into a task.

Drag everyone down with you

Misery loves company because nobody likes to take the fall alone. *Llevarse a todos entre las patas* = To drag everyone down with you (literally, "to carry everyone between the legs"). *Si ustedes me delatan con la policía, me voy a llevar a todos ustedes entre las patas* = If any of you rat on me to the police, I'm going to take all of you down with me.

Drag someone into the mess

At a family gathering you're minding your own business when out of nowhere you hear your name mentioned in someone else's conversation from across the room. *"No me saques a mí,"* you warn ("Don't drag me into the mess," "Don't involve me," or "Don't get me into this") from the verb *sacar*. You can also say, *"No me metas"* ("Don't get me involved" from the verb *meter*), but this usually implies that there is a problem or altercation and you don't want to be a part of it. Don't forget that the verb *sacar* is also employed in order to get something out of someone or to extract information from someone (like gossip). See "Fish for information" in this chapter.

Draw attention

Apantallar = To draw attention, to "wow," or make an impression on. It helps if you know that a *pantalla* is a screen (like a movie screen) because the movies are all about captivating an audience and sometimes making people believe something is more than it really is. Take, for example, those restaurant menus that contain mouth-watering pictures of the food entrees that look so much more delectable in the pictures than in reality. If you ordered what looked like gigantic prawns on the menu only to get a plate of guppy-sized shrimp, then you could complain, *"Pedí el plato de camarón porque cuando vi la foto en el menú me apantalló"* ("I asked for the shrimp plate because I was impressed by the picture of it on the menu.")

Empty

Most of us have learned that "empty" is *vacío*. This is true when you're talking about an empty cup or container. When referring to an empty place like a restaurant or club that has very few people inside, however, you will often hear *estar solo(a)* used instead. *El restaurante está solo. A lo mejor significa que la comida es mala* = This restaurant is empty. Maybe it means the food is bad.

Encourage, Egg on, Promote

The verb *fomentar* means to encourage, foster, and promote similar to how special-interest groups promote reading, staying in school, and saying no to drugs—all of which are noble and worthy causes. Sometimes, however, *fomentar* encourages unworthy causes or negative behavior. For example, it seems that every joke your boss tells is absolutely hilarious simply because the boss tells it. Now she thinks she's a real comedian and just won't stop, and at this point your facial muscles are already straining from pretending to laugh. You and your coworkers only have yourselves to blame. Next time, *no le fomentes* (Don't encourage or egg her on).

Errands

I include this one for practical purposes and not because it's such an eye-opening revelation, because it's not. Doing errands is just such a routine part of life that you'll need to know this phrase in everyday conversations. *Hacer mandados* = To do errands. *Este fin de semana tengo que hacer muchos mandados para mi esposa* = This weekend I have to do a lot of errands for my wife.

Fake, Phony

There are many ways to express being "fake" or "phony" in Spanish, whether it be a fake replica of a real person at the wax museum or a real person who is just insincere or phony. The adjective *falso(a)*, used with the verb *ser*, is the general way to express either. *Esta estatua se ve real pero es falsa* = This statue looks real but it's fake. As previously mentioned, *falso(a)* also applies to people whose sincerity you may question. *María se ve muy buena onda, pero en realidad es muy falsa* = Maria looks totally cool, but in reality she's very phony. You could even choose to tell María directly, *"¡Qué falsa eres!"* ("You're so phony!").

Ser de mentiras means "to be fake" (literally, "to be of lies") but it applies exclusively to fake objects that look real or lifelike but aren't—such as dolls, statues, and flowers, among other things. *Las flores de tu florero parecen de verdad, pero son de mentiras* = The flowers in your flower vase look real but they're fake. Note: *Ser de mentiras* does not apply to imitations such as an imitation of a brand name shirt, for example. For that, just use the noun *imitación.* The verb for "to fake," "to pretend," or "to make like" is *hacerse. Te hiciste el dormido pero escuchaste toda nuestra conversación* = You pretended to be asleep, but you heard our entire conversation. An exclamatory *¡No te hagas!* means "Don't even try to fake it!" which is said when your little brother plays as if he didn't know that last slice of pie he ate was actually for you. *Fingir* also means "to fake" or "to pretend." You can say, *"Fingiste muy bien"* ("You faked it really well") to that gold-digger who faked her love for her husband in order to benefit from his wealth. *Hacer la finta de* expresses "to fake like" but refers to a more physical type of fake similar to a basketball player who fakes the shot but passes the ball instead. *Eduardo hizo la finta de tirar, pero pasó la pelota al otro jugador* = Eduardo faked the shot but passed the ball to another player.

False

Naturally one might think that the Spanish word *falso(a)* would also be the perfect translation for the English "false." This is not true in the majority of cases. So when does *falso(a)* in Spanish actually equate to "false" in English? *Falso(a)* typically means false when referring to information and facts that are found to be untrue. *Lo que me dijo era falso* = What he told me was false (untrue).

Parapeto gives the idea of falseness as in a "false front" based on outward appearance. *Parapeto* is most often spoken in two ways: either with the verb *ser* as in *ser un parapeto,* or with the verb *estar* as in *estar de parapeto.* Both mean exactly the same thing—"It's just a front." So, one could say, *"Es un parapeto,"* or *"Está de parapeto"* about that restaurant that serves as a "front" for a money-laundering business, about that car that is in mint condition on the outside but can't outrun a lawnmower, or even about the lone bouncer standing outside the club used as a "front" to make it look like security is tight (when it's not). One could also comment, *"La tiene de parapeto"* ("He has her as a front") about that rich old man who has his much younger and beautiful girlfriend at his side as merely a trophy.

Postizo(a) also gives the idea of falseness but generally refers to false body parts, and by that I mean false eyelashes (*pestañas postizas*), false teeth (*dientes postizos*), false nails (*uñas postizas*), and even prosthetic limbs. *Esas pestañas postizas se ven naturales* = Those false eyelashes look natural.

Far away

This is another one of those "just thought you'd like to know" bits of information. *Estar lejos* is the standard for "to be far" or "to be far away," but you will also hear *estar retirado(a),* which means the same thing. *¿Qué tan lejos está tu casa de aquí?* (How far is your house from here?). *Está retirada* (It's far). To explain that something is "way the hell out there," you can use the very Mexican expression, *hasta la quinta chingada* (refer to *chingar* in chapter 6 for more details).

Find out

On spring break you and your friend are looking for a nice restaurant for dinner and you spot an interesting eatery. You ask your friend if it looks good. Uncertain if this is the right place, your friend walks towards the restaurant to get a better look inside and says, *"Averigüemos,"* which means "We'll see," "Let's see," or "Let's find out" from the verb *averiguar* (to find out). You can also use the more common and abbreviated *A ver* for "Let's see" (notice that *a ver* consists of the first four letters of the verb *averiguar*). *Vamos a ver qué hay de comer en este restaurante* = Let's see what kind of food this restaurant has. *Investigar* also means "to find out," but normally it has more of a research connotation to it. *Enterarse* means "to find out" but in the sense of discovering new information. *Me enteré que ellos se casaron en secreto* = I found out that they got married in secret.

Fish for information, Extract information

The best all-purpose way to express "fishing for information," "extracting information," or "getting something out of someone" is with the verb *sacar*. *Consuelo quería saber todo el chisme pero no iba a sacar nada de mí* = Consuelo wanted to know all the gossip but she wasn't going to get anything out of me. For those adventurous souls in need of a challenge, throw *meter aguja para sacar hebra* into the conversation and you might draw some *oohs* and *ahhs*. Literally, this expression means to stick in the needle (*aguja*) in order to pull out the thread (*hebra*). *Cuando Susana se enteró que yo tenía un secreto, trató de meter aguja para sacar hebra* = When Susana found out that I had a secret, she tried to wheedle it out of me.

Flatter

In Spanish the verbs for "to flatter" are *echar flores*, *dar piropos*, or *halagar*, but these are much more than verbs; it's an art if you can use these words to your advantage. *Carlos siempre les da piropos a las muchachas con quienes quiere salir* = Carlos always gives compliments to the girls with whom he wants to go out.

Flip for it (Flip a coin)

Trying to decide who's going to be the one to run to the market for more beer at halftime of the football game? Why not just do what the referee did to start the game and flip for it? *Echar un volado* is how you do it in Spanish. *Hay que echar un volado* = We should flip for it. In Spanish the equivalent for "heads or tails" is *cara o cruz*.

Flirt

Coquetear = To flirt. *Me sentí muy incómodo en la oficina porque mi jefa estaba coqueteando conmigo* = I felt very uncomfortable in the office because my boss was flirting with me. The reflexive form of *volar* (*volarse*) is also another good way to convey the same thing. *Laura se voló con un muchacho que conoció en el club* = Laura flirted with a guy she met at the club. Less formal but more hip are the close relatives of *coquetear—ligar* and *tirar la onda*. Both mean "to flirt" but since we did say they were more hip than their formal predecessor, *coquetear*, the better translation would be "to hit on," "to hook up with," "to bust a move on," or "to pick up on." *Mi primo Jesús les tira la onda a todas las mujeres en la discoteca, pero nunca tiene suerte* = My cousin Jesús hits on all the women at the disco, but he never has any luck.

Fool, Deceive

The verbs for "to fool" (someone) are *engañar, hacer trampas,* and *hacer trucos*—which all mean to fool, trick, or deceive. These expressions can explain how that shady used-car salesperson sold you the cleanest, shiniest piece of junk that broke down in a month. *Este vendedor de carros se quiere hacer el honesto pero nada más me está engañando* = This car salesman wants to make like he's honest but he's only deceiving me. *Hacer tonto(a),* or *hacer pendejo(a),* is how one expresses "making a fool of someone." Suppose you were to meet your blind date at the theater but she didn't show up and you're left standing in the rain with a bouquet of flowers and a bruised ego. Then not only did she stand you up (see, "Leave someone hanging" later in this chapter), but she also made a fool of you. *"¡Me hizo tonto!"* ("She made a fool of me!"), you explain to your friends when you arrive back home.

For free, For nothing

The word "free" is like music to the ears … unless of course you're referring to the free piano lessons I received from my mother's friend. At the expense of my pride, this example leads us to to the difference between "for free" and "for nothing." In many instances, there is no difference. If you receive free food from the grand opening of the new taco stand, then you also got it for nothing. Sometimes, however, we say, "for free" (without cost) when we really mean to say, "for nothing" (in vain). Something that is free (without cost) is *gratis* or *gratuito*. Something that is done in vain or for nothing (without results) is done *de oquis, en balde,* or *en vano. La amiga de mi mamá me dio lecciones de piano de oquis porque nunca aprendí* = My mother's friend gave me piano lessons for nothing (in vain) because I never learned anything. Using the same example, the following would also be true: *La amiga de mi mamá me dio lecciones de piano gratis* = My mother's friend gave me free piano lessons (because we didn't pay).

If something is being given away for free (free Thanksgiving turkeys at the local market or free food at the neighborhood block party), then use the expression *ir al garrote* (to go to the "free-for-all") to express your intent to take full advantage of the freebee. Let's say that the local supermarket was advertising free groceries (first-come, first-serve) on everything in the entire store from 2:00 until 2:30. That's when you tell your starving student friends, *"¡Vamos al garrote!"* ("Let's go to the free-for-all").

Full of surprises

You and your husband finally decide to take your first vacation from Nowhereville, U.S.A., to Guadalajara, Mexico. Upon arrival, you are shocked to find your husband speaking fluently in Spanish with the locals. Maybe it's because you never asked, or maybe it's because he had no opportunities to speak Spanish back in your hometown, Nowhereville, U.S.A. You may have thought you knew everything about him but *él es un estuche de monerías* (He's a box full of suprises).

Get along

Llevarse bien, acoplarse bien, and *compaginar bien* all mean "to get along." Use any of them interchangeably to describe how you get along (or not get along) with someone. *Nos llevamos bien, nos acoplamos bien,* and *compaginamos bien* all mean "We get along well." Add *no* before these verbs and you have the opposite. *Mi primo y yo no compaginamos muy bien* = My cousin and I don't get along really well.

Get angry, Get pissed off

There are several ways to express "to get angry" or "to get pissed off" in Spanish. The most common is *enojarse. No te enojes porque siempre gano* = Don't get angry just because I always win. Then there's the very Mexican expression *dar coraje,* which leans more towards "getting pissed off" than getting angry. *Me dio mucho coraje cuando me pegó* = It really pissed me off when he hit me. Also in wide circulation is the less refined and more slangy *encabronarse. Mi amigo se encabronó mucho cuando a la última hora le dije que yo tenía que cancelar nuestra cita* = My friend got very pissed when at the last minute I told him that I had to cancel our appointment. If you're extremely pissed and the shit has just hit the fan, then the verbal expression *cagar la madre* (literally, "to shit the mother") may more accurately express your anger; however, it is hardly appropriate in most situations because it is a bit *corriente* (low-class). Stay clear of using it if you can (for an example of the usage, see "*Madre*" in chapter 6).

If these expressions do not quite express the intensity of your feelings, then maybe the expression you're looking for is *poner el grito en el cielo*, which literally means "to scream to the heavens" but may be more commonly recognized as "to throw a fit." *¡Cuando mamá se entere de que rompiste la ventana, va a poner el grito en el cielo!* = When Mom finds out that you broke the window, she's going to throw a fit!

Get away with something, Get one's way

"To get away with something" and "to get one's way" are both expressed with *salirse con la suya*. That thug Fredo who robs banks and doesn't get caught is an example of someone who gets away with things. *Los rateros han robado tres bancos y siempre se han salido con la suya porque hasta hoy no los han agarrado* = The thieves have robbed three banks and each time they have gotten away with it because they haven't caught them yet. "To get one's way" is a very different expression but, as mentioned, it is also expressed with *salirse con la suya*. Here's an example. If your wife always asks you where you want to eat but you always end up going where she wants, then you could say, *"¿Por qué me preguntas dónde quiero comer si al final siempre te sales con la tuya?"* ("Why do you ask me where I want to eat if in the end you always get your way?").

Get hooked, Get addicted

Sex, drugs, food, love . . . , whatever it is, we all have our addictions regardless of how slight they may be. *Estar adicto(a)* means "to *be* hooked or addicted." *Mi amigo está adicto al café* = My friend is addicted to coffee. *Picarse* means "to get (not be) hooked or addicted" and can be used for addictions of any sort—good, bad, or neutral, such as an addiction to gambling, drugs, love, sweets, you name it. For vices and addictions that are generally considered bad (gambling, smoking, drugs, etc.), you can use *enviciarse*, though as previously mentioned, you can always use the more general *picarse*. Before hitting the blackjack tables in Las Vegas, you may warn your friend by telling him, *"Ten cuidado porque te envicias"* or *"Ten cuidado porque te picas"* ("Be careful because you can get hooked").

Get into a jam, Be behind the eight ball

Ponerse la soga al cuello literally means "to put the noose to the neck." It is the equivalent of how we say in English "to be behind the eight ball," "to hang oneself," or "to get into a real jam." Sometimes the expressions for getting into problems (*meterse en problemas* or *meterse en líos*) don't sufficiently illustrate what kind of bind you may be in. *Ponerse la soga al cuello*, however, means to get into a jam to the point where you are at the end of the rope and in a "do-or-die" situation. Suppose you're applying for a job that you know will be high stress, take all your free time away, and virtually eliminate your social life. With all this in mind, your best friend tells you, *"Si aceptas ese trabajo tú solo te estás poniendo la soga al cuello,"* which translates to "If you take that job, you're the one hanging yourself."

Get old, hackneyed, trite

Estar choteado(a) = To get old but it has nothing to do with age. It means that something has worn out its novelty. Popular songs that are overplayed on the radio, or the new designer shoes that are not so original anymore because the whole world seems to own a pair, are examples of *cosas que están choteadas* (things that have worn out their novelty). *El vestido azul está muy choteado … mejor me pongo el rojo* = The blue dress has been overworn … I'd better wear the red one. Also, see *¡Ya chole!* in chapter 9.

Get the better of, Get the best of

The verb *ganar* means to beat, defeat, or win. *Ganar*, however, also means "to get the better of" or "to get the best of." For example, if you failed to hold back those tears while watching a tearjerker movie with your girlfriend, then she might tell you, *"Te ganó el sentimiento."* This translates to "Your feelings got the better of you" or "That movie really got to you." Of course, anything can get the better of you—a propensity to lie, to be greedy, or to have bad habits. *Pedro no puede dejar de fumar. Le ganó el vicio* = Pedro can't stop smoking. His bad habit got the better of him.

Get the hang of

The hip way to say, "to get the hang of" is *agarrar la onda* (to catch the drift). After several surfing lessons you're finally able to stand up on the board. *"¡Agarré la onda!"* ("I got it!" or "I got the hang of it!"), you proudly tell your instructor. *Agarrar el truco* (to get the trick) also means "to get the hang of" but can imply that there was a trick or twist to it. *Ya le agarré el truco a la cámara digital porque estaba muy complicada* = I finally got the trick to the digital camera because it was really complicated. If you want to go by the book, then *aprender* (to learn) might be your preference, but everyone knows this one already. I would urge you to consider using *agarrar la onda* or *agarrar el truco* when called for because although slang, they are fast becoming the standard.

Give a piece of your mind

Have you ever been pissed off or annoyed at someone to the point where you just had to give the person a piece of your mind? Should such an occasion arise, *decirle a alguien sus cuatro verdades* is the expression you need to use to explain how you told your boss what you really thought of him (yeah, right). The literal meaning is "to tell someone his or her four truths" (but of course you may need to tell more than that). It means "to give someone a piece of your mind" or "to tell someone off." *Julio siempre es grosero conmigo. La próxima vez le voy a decir sus cuatro verdades* = Julio is always rude to me. Next time I'm going to give him a piece of my mind.

Give it all you've got

Echar toda la carne al asador (literally, "to throw all the meat on the grill") = To give it all you've got. It means to put your heart and soul into something. A football coach who tells his players to leave their hearts and guts on the field is essentially motivating them to play with every ounce of energy possible. *Éste es el juego del campeonato, así que tienen que echar toda la carne al asador* = It's the championship game, so you have to lay it all out on the line.

Give up

Though I don't recommend that you do this while reading this book, expressing "giving up" in Spanish is relatively easy. *Rendirse* or *darse por vencido* = To give up. *Darse por vencido*, however, is often shortened to *darse*. Thus, "I give up" is frequently heard as *"Me doy"* or *"Me rindo."* *Víctor nunca se rinde. Todavía persigue a Selena* = Víctor never gives up. He's still pursuing Selena.

Glimpse through, Flip through

If you know that *una hoja* is a page or piece of paper, then you won't have any trouble remembering that "to glimpse through" or "flip through" a book or magazine, for example, is *hojear*. *Voy a hojear la revista porque no tengo tiempo de leerla toda* = I'm going to flip through the magazine because I don't have time to read the whole thing.

Go against someone

To "go against" somebody is expressed with *dar la contra* (literally, to "give the opposite"). Parents may tell their rebellious teenage son, *"¿Por qué siempre nos das la contra?"* ("Why do you always go against us?") *Tener algo en contra de* = To have something against (someone or something). *No tengo nada en contra de nadie* = I don't have anything against anyone.

Go clubbing

I've always pondered the origins of the term "clubbing." For some reason, I see images of prehistoric cavemen at the local cave-rave "clubbing" their love interests and dragging them back to the cave. Who knows, but better to leave this up to historians. *Ir al club* or *ir a la discoteca* are universally understood, but the trendy term for "to go clubbing" is *ir de antro*. *Nos vamos de antro* = Let's go clubbing. The term *antro* is widely used among the younger party people of Mexico but may not be understood in all Spanish-speaking countries, in which case you can always fall back on *ir al club* or *ir a la discoteca*.

Go from bad to worse

Ir de mal en peor = To go from bad to worse. You would say, *"Fue de mal en peor"* about your health after your case of sniffles turned into a full-blown flu. There are, however, a few other related expressions that you should learn. *Estar del remate* means "to get worse" but does not necessarily mean that things were bad to begin with. It could refer to your voice, performance in school, driving skills, and even your dog's behavior of late. *No puedo controlar a mi perro. Está del remate* = I can't control my dog. He's getting worse. *Llover sobre mojado* is a handy expression when it's just one of those days when nothing seems to go right. You're walking home and step in a deep puddle of mud. Then you step in gum with your other foot. To top it all off, when you finally get home, your own dog takes a leak on your leg. As you enter the door, your mother asks, "How was your day?" You might say, *"Me ha llovido sobre mojado,"* which is to say, "When it rains, it pours," or "One bad thing happened after another."

Go to one's head

Some say that success breeds contempt. Maybe part of the reason is because we so often let it go to our heads. *Subirse a la cabeza* = To go to one's head, and it usually means that success has changed you in some way (mostly negatively). *Nomar era más humilde antes de que su taquería llegara a tener fama. Ahora todo el dinero se le ha subido a la cabeza* = Nomar was more humble before his *taquería* became famous. Now all that money has really gone to his head. *Estás guapo(a), pero no dejes que se te suba a la cabeza* = You're good-looking, but don't let it get to your head.

Go with the flow, Go along with

Seguir el rollo or *seguir la corriente* (you can use either) both mean "to go with the flow," "to go along with," or "to roll with the punches." *Me gusta andar con Juan porque siempre sigue el rollo* = I like to hang out with Juan because he always goes with the flow. Another good expression is *dorar la píldora* (to sugarcoat the pill). It is similar to the other two, but there is a difference. *Dorar la píldora* hints at actively "playing along with" or "humoring" someone. It conveys a more purposeful intention than the laid back "just let it be" feeling of *seguir el rollo* and *seguir la corriente*. *Los chistes de mi jefa no me dan risa, pero no más le doro la píldora* = My boss's jokes aren't funny, but I just "humor her," or play along with her.

Guess

The serious student of the language will eventually have to become familiar with the different ways "to guess" is used. The differences can be very subtle, so it is important that you learn them well, and better now so you don't have to guess later. *Adivinar* is the correct choice for guessing in general. Someone asks how old you are. *"Adivina"* ("Guess"), you reply. "Guess what?" is *¿Adivina qué?* but even more common for "Guess what?" is *¿Qué crees? Atinarle* means more or less "to guess right." It is used somewhat playfully and informally like when guessing how many fingers someone is holding behind her back or when guessing how many jellybeans are in the jar. Suppose your nephew asks for an action figure for his birthday. You buy one but you're not sure if it's the exact one he wanted. When your nephew opens the gift, you can ask, *"¿Le atiné al regalo?"* ("Did I guess the right gift?"). *Acertar* is very similar to *atinarle*. The difference is that *acertar* is used in a more formal and serious manner. With *acertar*, the emphasis is less on *guessing* something correct and more on *getting* something correct. For example, your teacher asks the class a question and then says, *"A ver si le aciertas"* ("Let's see if you get it"), pointing to you for an answer. Here, you're not really being asked to *guess* the answer correctly. You're being asked to *get* the answer correct.

Handy

In Spanish, to have something physically handy or convenient is to have it *a la mano*. *Guardar a la mano* is "to keep something handy." *Guarda tu dinero a la mano por si lo ocupas* = Keep your money handy in case you need it. *Estar a la mano* is used when describing something that is physically close by or handy like that nearby convenience store or hospital. *El área donde vivimos me gusta porque el hospital está a la mano* = I like the area where we live because the hospital is so close by (handy).

Have nothing to do with

Defending oneself is a natual instinct, but doing it in another language is not always so easy. What would you say if your classmate got caught cheating on his exam because somebody ratted him out and he unjustly blamed it on you? You might throw your hands up and say, "I had nothing to do with it!" Well, you do the same in Spanish except you say, *"¡No tenía nada que ver con eso!"* It comes from *no tener nada que ver con*, which means "to not have anything to do with." Now suppose his main reason for blaming you was because you were the last one out of the classroom. *"¿Qué tiene que ver eso?"* might be your next response ("What does that have to do with it?").

Have pull (influence)

Powerful, famous, and even good-paying customers often have "pull" in many of the places they patronize, and though we sometimes despise them for receiving special treatment, we common folk would switch places with them in a heartbeat if we could. *Tener palanca* literally translates to "to have pull," since a *palanca* is any lever that can be pulled. *No hicimos reservaciones para comer en este restaurante, pero no te preocupes porque tengo mucha palanca aquí* = We didn't make reservations to eat at this restaurant, but don't worry because I have a lot of pull here.

Have someone all figured out

We already know that *manejar* means to drive. Figuratively, however, *manejar* can be used in the expression *tener a alguien bien manejado(a)*, meaning to have someone all figured out, well managed, and under control. It means that you know someone's MO (*modus operandi*). That is, you know what makes the person tick or what his or her intentions, motives, and reactions might be, thus giving you the inside scoop or the upper hand. For example, daddy's little girl might have her overprotective father *bien manejado* in order to get what she wants. *Yo sé como manejar a mi papá para que me dé permiso para salir* = I know how to manage my dad so that he lets me go out.

Have someone on a short leash

Tener alguien cortito(a) = To have someone on a short leash. Perhaps it's a trust issue or perhaps a jealousy issue. In any case, some wives may have flirtatious husbands on a short leash the same way one might put a dog in heat on a short leash. *Carla tiene a su esposo bien cortito y no lo dejó ir a la despedida de soltero* = Carla has her husband on a short leash and she didn't let him go to the bachelor party.

Have the chance (opportunity)

The easy way to say, "to have the chance" (opportunity) is *tener chanza* or *tener oportunidad*. Both are correct but let's remember that this book is not about teaching you the easiest way to say or remember words in Spanish. This book is about teaching you the best way to say things. That is, it's about illustrating the most common ways things are said among native speakers. For that reason, you must also learn the verb *tocar*. *Tocar* means "to touch" and it also means "to play" (an instrument), but more significantly, it is a good way to say, "to have the chance or opportunity." When someone asks if you saw the new action movie that just came out, you say, *"No me ha tocado"* ("I haven't had the chance") if you haven't, and *"Sí, ya me tocó verla,"* if you have. While we're on the subject, it is important to note that the verb *tocar* is also how native speakers express "to be one's turn." *Ahora me toca cuidar a mi abuelita* = Now it's my turn to take care of my grandmother.

Hint

Dar una pista = To give a hint (clue). Your friend says, *"¿Adivina a quién vi esta mañana?"* ("Guess who I saw this morning?"). Before you give up, say, *"Dame una pista"* ("Give me a hint"). *Dar una indirecta* (and *tirar una indirecta*) also mean "to give a hint" but more for the purposes of getting one's point across. For example, Víctor is in hot pursuit of Selena in spite of all of the deflating hints (*indirectas*) that she unabashedly gives him: When Víctor shows up, Selena leaves; when he calls, she hangs up; and when he waves hello, she waves back (with her middle finger). *Selena le dio muchas indirectas a Víctor pero él sigue persiguiéndola* = Selena gave a lot of hints to Víctor, but he keeps pursuing her.

Hip, Trendy, In fashion, In style

Estar de moda and *andar a la última moda* mean to be "hip," "trendy," and up to the latest in fashion or style. *Manuel siempre anda a la última moda* = Manuel is always in fashion. It is often quite surprising and even shocking to know some of the silly fashions that are considered to be trendy today. I guess it is just as well that things go out of fashion as quickly as they come into fashion. Being "out of fashion" is expressed with *estar desmodado(a)* or *andar desmodado(a)*. *La camisa de mi papá estaba de moda antes, pero ahora está desmodada* = My father's shirt was in style before, but now it's out of style.

Hit someone where it hurts

If you're a man, we all know where this spot is, but let's not be so one-track-minded. To "hit someone where it hurts most" (*dar en donde más le duele*) is not limited to body parts. For example, you could get a hefty speeding ticket when you're already in a terrible financial crunch. *La patrulla me dio en donde más me duele—en la cartera* = The police hit me where it hurts most—in the wallet.

Hog, Hoard

Acapararse, posesionarse, aborazarse, and *engolosinarse* all mean to hog or hoard. *Aborazarse* and *engolosinarse* are typically said for hogging food (particularly sweets like candy, cakes, cookies, and chips, for example) and implies a mild addiction seemingly beyond one's control. It's sort of like how when one opens a bag of one's favorite cookies and just can't help but finish off the bag. *Siempre te engolosinas con las galletas y no me dejas nada* = You always hog all the cookies and you don't leave me any. *Es un bufet, así que no te aboraces con la comida* = It's a buffet, so don't hoard the food.

The other two (*acapararse* and *posesionarse*) are said for hogging or hoarding everything else. *¿Por qué siempre quieres acaparar toda la atención de la gente?* = Why do you always want to hog all the attention from everyone? *Te acaparas tanto de la tele que yo no puedo ver nada* = You hog the TV so much that I can't watch anything. Finally, to your friend who's hogging the mike at the karaoke bar, you can say, *"No te posesiones del micrófono. ¡Queremos cantar también!"* ("Don't hog the mike. We want to sing, too!").

Hold a grudge

Tener rencor = To hold a grudge. It is often the culprit of strained relationships and long, grueling hours of the silent treatment. After getting into a big argument, you and your friend haven't spoken to each other for days until one of you finally breaks the silence by saying, "*No me tengas rencor para siempre*" ("Don't hold a grudge against me forever"). Along the same lines, another verb worthy of your attention is *entercarse* (to get stubborn). *No me gusta pelear contigo porque siempre te entercas muy feo* = I don't like to argue with you because you always get so damn stubborn.

Hold back, Restrain oneself

Detenerse = To hold back, but just as it is in English, Spanish speakers use it more often in the negative expression "not to hold back" (*no detenerse*). It is used most frequently to describe people's inability to restrain or control themselves. *Cuando Benito está enojado, no se detiene. Te dice todo lo que piensa* = When Benito is angry, he doesn't hold back. He tells you whatever he thinks.

Hold one's own

Suppose someone asks if you can speak Spanish or if you're any good at baseball or if you're a good dancer. If your answer is closer to yes than no (or if you really are good but too modest to admit it), then you could say, "*Me defiendo*" (from the verb *defenderse*), which translates to "I hold my own," "I manage," or "I get by."

Hype up (with the verb "get"), Get jazzed

Alborotar = To get hyped up, jazzed, or excited with anticipation. Let's say you told your girlfriend last month that you were going to take her to see her favorite singer in concert. Suddenly, the day before the concert you break the news that you won't be able to go. She then tells you, "*¡Ya me habías alborotado, rajón!*" ("You already had me all excited and hyped up, you flake!"). If you tell your baby daughter that you'll buy her an ice cream but then realize that you don't have time, then your wife may sympathetically say, "*¡Ya la alborotaste!*" ("Now you got her all hyped up!"). Or suppose it's time for your daughter to go to sleep and you start tickling her when you really should be reading her a bedtime story. Your wife might warn, "*¡No la alborotes!*" ("Don't get her all hyped up!").

In the same boat (situation)

Estar en la misma (literally, "to be in the same") = To be in the same boat (situation). I can only assume that this expression in English originated long ago somewhere at sea and probably in a crowded boat with miserable conditions. Since then, this expression has come ashore but no matter where we are, the boat analogy has stuck with us. The Spanish version of this expression gets rid of the boat altogether, but the meaning is the same. You and your cousin Jaime are both standing on a crowded bus, face to face with six pairs of sweaty armpits on all sides. Jaime can't stop complaining about the stench, so you shut him up with, *"¡No te quejes porque estamos en la misma!"* ("Stop complaining because we're all in the same boat").

In the way

Depending on how polite or rude you choose to be and also depending on to whom you're talking, you can take your pick on the many ways to let people know they're in your way. If you're watching television and your grandmother is directly in your line of vision, you might politely say, *"Con permiso"* ("With your permission") and she'll move out of your way without a fuss. *Con permiso* is always the polite form. *Estás en mi camino* or *Me estorbas* both mean "You're in my way," and these expressions are a little rude unless of course preceded by the words *con permiso.* To your little bratty brother you might raise your voice a few decibels and impatiently yell, *"¡Quítate!"* for "Get out of the way!" *"¿Te tapo?"* from the verb *tapar* (to block) means "Am I blocking you?" Saving the best for last, you can say, *"La carne de burro no es transparente,"* which means "Donkey meat isn't transparent." This is a humorous phrase but only if you address it to the right person. So, unless you're actually talking to a donkey, make sure you are either joking or that you have a good relationship with the person to whom you say this. Otherwise, someone's fist might be in the way of your face.

In the works, In progress, Pending

Seguir en trámite or *estar en trámite* = To be "in the works," to be "in process," or to be "pending." These verbs describe pending paperwork (reports, lawsuits, permits, DMV renewals, etc.) that may be pending approval, denial, processing, and so on. *Mis papeles de inmigración están en trámite todavía* = My immigration papers are still pending. When the boss asks about that report he needed by yesterday, you can reply, *"Sigue en trámite*" ("I'm working on it"). Though clever but unconventional, you can also use *seguir en trámite* or *estar en trámite* to describe your progress with that gal or guy you've been pursuing. "*Oye, Susette, qué pasa con ese muchacho que estás persiguiendo?*" ("Hey, Susette, what's going on with that guy that you're pursuing?"). Susette responds with, "*Sigue en trámite*" or "*Está en trámite*" for "He's still in the works" or "I'm working on him."

Infatuated

Encapricharse con = To be infatuated with. If Susana is infatuated with Pablo, it means that she has a crush on him. It means that she "digs him," fancies him, or is stuck on him. *Susana se encaprichó con Pablo cuando lo conoció* = Susana became infatuated with Pablo when she met him. *Encaprichar en* (in the nonreflexive form) means "to obsess about" or "to have one's mind made up" about something (not someone). *Claudia está encaprichada en ir a Europa aun si sus padres no la dejan* = Claudia is obsessed about going to Europe even if her parents don't let her.

Jinx

Don't you sometimes feel that when someone warns you about something and later that "something" actually happens, that the person jinxed you? For example, everyone in your family got sick except you. Your friend then tells you how lucky you are for always being so healthy. Shortly after that comment you start to feel a little queasy and then you start vomiting. "*¡Me echaste la sal!*" you say accusingly ("You jinxed me!"). This comes from the expression *echar la sal*, which literally means "to throw the salt." In conversation, however, it means, "to jinx" or "to give bad luck." You know your friend's words (which were well intentioned) didn't actually induce your vomiting, but you feel that they created a negative energy and were at least partly responsible for your getting sick. Along the same lines, *estar salado(a)* (literally, "to be salty") means "to be unlucky" or "to be jinxed." After losing five times in a row at the blackjack table, you leave and warn others, "*Esta mesa está salada*" ("This table is bad luck" or "This table is jinxed").

Joke around

To joke around is *bromear* or *vacilar*. "I'm joking" is *Estoy bromeando* or *Estoy vacilando*, and "It's a joke" is *Es una broma*. On many occasions, however, the quicker and easier *¡Mentiras!* will be the more appropriate, less cumbersome response. Yes, *mentiras* means "lies" and perhaps you weren't lying, but only joking. Well, relax because nobody is calling you a liar. In certain contexts it's just another way of saying, "Just kidding!" For example, you might tell your friend that you saw his girlfriend with another guy over the weekend, then wait for his jaw to drop and his eyes to pop out before you finally proclaim, "*¡Mentiras!*" ("Just kidding!").

Manchar and *mamar* are the younger relatives of *bromear* and *vacilar*. I say younger because these verbs are more commonly spoken among the younger generation. Both are used in the negative to say, "Don't even joke about it!" "Don't mess around!" or "No freakin' way!" Let's say your name was picked from thousands of names in the raffle drawing and you've just won a new, fully equipped Mercedes Benz. With a stunned expression, you might say, "*¡No manches!*" or "*¡No mames!*" Here's another example for good measure: You and your friends are trying to get to the other side of a fifteen-foot wall. Someone suggests, "Let's climb up and jump down." The rest of you answer with a definitive, "*¡No mames!*" ("Don't even joke about it," "No way!" or "Not even!").

Kick someone out

Correr is "to run" but it also means to "kick someone out" or "throw someone out." The last customer in the store could safely assume, *Me están corriendo* (They're throwing me out) when the employees turn off all the lights, close the register, and open the front door for him without his asking.

Kick someone's ass

To kick someone's ass (beat up on someone) is not appropriate behavior unless absolutely justified (and sometimes it really is), but I don't condone anyone using this phrase in an abusive manner, if at all. I include it because it exists in real conversation though for good reason you won't hear it too often. I also include it because if you hear it said to you, it means that you should probably run for your life. *Te voy a meter unos chingadazos* (from *meter unos chingadazos*) = "I'm going to kick your ass." Spoken lightheartedly, you may elicit a few laughs, but it's most likely because you are afforded a little more latitude since Spanish is not your native tongue. Otherwise, I would steer clear of this one even if there were only a slight chance of someone taking you seriously. Keep in mind that the verb *chingar* is a very common Mexican term. In other parts of Central America, you may hear the expression *dar un vergazo* for "to kick someone's ass."

Kill the mood

To "kill the mood" or "shoot down a great idea" can be expressed with *cortar el avión*. Literally, it means to "cut the airplane" but it is only a figure of speech for a great idea or a mood flying high only to be suddenly cut short. For example, you're in the house watching television with your buddies when one of them mentions getting some mouth-watering *tacos de carne asada*. Without much deliberation everyone gets up and bolts towards the door for the nearest *taquería*. That is … until you explain that the nearest *taquería* is at least a half hour away. *"Nos cortaste el avión"* ("You killed that idea"), they moan. Let's look at another example. The comedian of the group, Fernando, has everyone rolling in laughter with one of his hilarious jokes. Then the awkward and off-the-wall Miguel (not known for his sense of humor) tries to add on to the joke with one of his own comments, and the roaring laughter comes to a sudden halt. *"¡Nos cortaste el avión!"* the group tells him.

Kill time

Time flies, but when it doesn't fly fast enough, sometimes you have to kill it. "To kill time" in English is pretty much a direct translation in Spanish— *matar el rato, matar el tiempo,* or *pasar el rato*. You're dropping your sister off to her violin lesson and since you have nothing to do until she finishes, you tell her, *"Voy a ir a la biblioteca a matar el rato"* ("I'm going to the library to kill time").

Kiss up to someone

To "kiss up," "suck up," "brown-nose," or "kiss-ass" is *hacer la barba*. *¡Mira a Juan haciendo la barba al maestro para que le ponga buenas calificaciones!* = Look at Juan kissing up to the teacher so that he gets good grades! The one doing the "kissing" would be called a *barbero(a)* or *lambiscón(a)*.

Lay all your cards on the table

To lay all your cards on the table is *poner todas las cartas sobre la mesa*. As the phrase suggests, it requires one to reveal one's entire hand in order to settle a matter or get to the bottom of something. Before getting married, Brenda told her financé, Marco, *"Mejor poner todas las cartas sobre la mesa para que no haya malentendidos"* ("It's better to lay all the cards on the table so that there are no misunderstandings"). In other words, Brenda is telling Marco to empty all of the skeletons from his closet so she won't encounter any surprising secrets several years into their marriage.

Learn from one's mistakes

Driving home from work, Lupe "Left Turn" López mistakenly makes a left turn on Elm Street instead of a right turn. The next day she did the same thing. The next day? You guessed it … she made the same mistake. It could be that she has problems with her short-term memory or simply that *Lupe no escarmienta* (Lupe doesn't learn from her mistakes) from the verb *escarmentar* (to learn from one's mistakes).

Least suitable person, Most suitable person

To be the least suitable person = *Ser el menos indicado* if referring to a male, and *ser la menos indicada* if referring to a female. This expression is directed at people who are not the appropriate individuals to give their contributions or to ask for favors either because it would seem hypocritical or because these individuals are not qualified. For example, if Sandra never helps out and never lifts a finger for anyone but herself, then when she asks for volunteers to help her in her moment of need, everyone might deny her on the grounds that she is the least suitable one to ask *(es la menos indicada)*. In the context of this example, this phrase translates to "She's the last person who has the right to ask for help." Another example would be that compulsive liar who tells everyone else not to lie. Well, since most of us tend to take advice more seriously from people who practice what they preach, one could reply with, *"Tú eres el menos indicado en darme un consejo porque siempre mientes"* ("You're the last person who should give me advice because you always lie").

If you want to express that someone is the *most* suitable or appropriate person for whatever situation is at hand, then just change the *menos* to *más*. For example, let's suppose you went on a vacation to Mexico with a group who only spoke English and you were the only one who spoke Spanish. Your friends might elect you as the spokesperson to order all the food, make all the tour reservations, and bargain down all the souvenir prices because *tú eres el más indicado* (You're the most suitable person or the best person for the task).

Leave someone hanging

To leave someone hanging = *Dejar chiflando en la loma* (literally, "to leave someone whistling on the hill") or *dejar a alguien plantado* (to leave someone high and dry). *Esperé en el café por una hora hasta que me di cuenta que ella me dejó chiflando en la loma* (or *me dejó plantado)* = I waited at the café for an hour before I realized she stood me up. In this example, "to leave someone hanging" also means "to stand someone up" for an appointment or a date, for example. If you leave someone hanging in suspense, then use *dejar picado*, which literally means to leave someone with a bite or itch (just waiting to be scratched). Suppose your friend starts to tell you some juicy gossip but doesn't finish the story because he has to pick up his son from school. You can tell him, "*¡No me dejes picado!*" ("Don't leave me hanging in suspense!").

Let oneself go

Oftentimes our inhibitions and timidness get the better of us, preventing us from performing to our full potential or from just being ourselves. For example, there are always some people at the disco who never make it to the dance floor because they claim they don't know how to dance. It's usually because they don't let themselves loosen up. Next time, tell them, "*¡Déjate llevar por la música!*" That is to say, "Relax and let yourself go with the music!" from the verb *dejarse llevar* (to let oneself go). Keep in mind that generally, you can simply say, "*Déjate llevar*" ("Let yourself go") by itself as long as the reference is clear.

Look down on

Snobs and other self-proclaimed VIPs tend to do this a lot. That is, they look down on or belittle others because somehow it got into their heads that they are better than the rest. *Despreciar* is the verb for this in Spanish. *Ana se cree mucho ... desprecia a toda la gente* = Ana thinks she's so important ... she looks down on everyone. (Also see "Think too highly of oneself" later in this chapter.)

Look out of the corner of one's eye

This one is often the source of a lot of confusion, so let's clear it up right now. Though the tendency to translate "I saw him out of the corner of my eye" is *Lo vi de la esquina de mi ojo,* this assertion is incorrect. The correct way to say, "I saw him out of the corner of my eye" is *"Lo vi de reojo"* from *ver de reojo.* While we're here, we might as well round out the other corners. *Rincón* is a corner of a room; *esquina* can also be said for a corner of the room as well as a street corner; and *orilla* is the edge or corner of a table, counter, or even the edge of the sea (shore), for example.

Loud

Most of us know that the adjectives to describe a loud noise are *ruidoso(a)*, *recio*, or *fuerte*, but what kind of "loud" describes that bright fluorescent yellow shirt with matching pants and hat? The word is *llamativo(a)*. Remember from Spanish 101 that "to call" is *llamar*, so it should be easy to remember that something that is *llamativo(a)* "calls" and sometimes screams for attention.

Make a big deal, fuss, or stink

Hacer mucho polvo = To make a big deal or fuss of something. Crying over who gets to sit in the front seat on a short drive to the market would be considered making a big deal of something (or nothing, depending on how you see it). *Hacer el pedo gordo* (literally, "to make the fat fart") is more than just something some people do after a large meal. In Spanish it is a humorous expression meaning "to make a stink, calamity, or commotion." If your house is the site of a heated argument, fight, or other ruckus, you can say, *"Aquí está el pedo gordo"* (referring to your house, of course). This expression translates to "Here's where all the commotion is," or "This is where the shit is happening."

Make a habit of

It's only your first week at your new job and you've been late every day so far. Unless you are the boss, your superior might tell you, *"No hagas costumbre de llegar tarde a la oficina"* ("Don't make a habit of arriving late to work") from *hacer costumbre de* (to make a habit of). To have a bad habit is *tener mala maña*. *Él tiene la mala maña de morderse las uñas cuando está nervioso* = He has a bad habit of biting his nails when he's nervous.

Make a killing

Hacer su agosto = To make a killing. Don't panic. There is no wild hunting tale or murderous horror story behind this expression. It actually refers more to making a substantial monetary acquisition or other type of beneficial gain. The lucky gambler who hit an outrageous hot streak, the new movie that broke one-hundred-million dollars on opening weekend, and the charity event that unexpectedly brought in donors by the thousands are examples of "making a killing." *Alfredo vende ropa en la pulga y hace su agosto* = Alfredo sells clothes at the flea market and makes a killing.

Make faces

Hacer caras = To make faces. This is something kids do all the time when teasing one another. Mother might say, *"¡No hagan caras!"* ("Don't make faces!") to her children at the dinner table, but perhaps what she hasn't realized is that the pained expressions on their faces are a result of her less-than-edible cooking.

Make someone beg, Play hardball

Hacerse del rogar = To make someone beg, to play hardball. Your friend Pedro loves to go clubbing every weekend but always pretends that he doesn't. The problem is that he doesn't want to have the clubbing-is-my-life reputation. It's only after you beg that he finally "relents," even if everyone already knew he was dying to go all along. *Pedro siempre se hace del rogar* = Pedro always makes you beg. See close relative "Play hard to get" (*darse a desear*) in this chapter.

Make someone suspicious

Your cousin introduces you to a guy who's wearing a nice leather jacket with the magnetic theft-prevention device still attached and he just bought everyone lunch with a credit card bearing the name and picture of a woman named Lola. Since you doubt this guy's name is Lola, your first thought might be, *No quiero andar con él porque me da mala espina* (I don't want to hang out with him because he makes me suspicious) from the expression *dar mala espina* (to make suspicious), which literally translates as "to give a bad thorn."

Meet up with someone

Nothing groundbreaking here but for some reason people always seem to have a hard time with it. To "meet up" with someone is commonly expressed by using *verse*—the reflexive form of the verb *ver* (to see). *Nos vemos en el café* = Let's meet at the café. *Veme en mi casa* = Meet me at my house. The verb *encontrar* is also good if you don't mind putting in the extra effort in pronunciation. *La encontré en el mercado* = I met up with her in the market.

Miss out on

¡No se pierda la venta de verano! (Don't miss out on the summer sale!). If you've watched enough Spanish-language television, then you've probably already heard this phrase in one of the commercials. "To miss out on" or "to lose out on" is *perderse*. *Te perdiste una buena cena en casa de Luisa* = You missed out on a great dinner at Luisa's house. *Te vas a perder la fiesta* is "You're going to miss out on the party." If it is already understood what is being missed (*la fiesta*, in this example) from the context of the conversation, then one could say, *"Te la vas a perder"* instead (the direct object *"la"* representing *"la fiesta"*). While we're on the subject, you should know that *perderse* is also the verb for "to get lost" or "to lose your way." So, after giving your cousin Fabio the directions to the party, tell him, *"No te pierdas"* ("Don't get lost").

Moods

Andar de buenas/malas = To be in a good/bad mood. *Mi jefe anda de buenas porque sus acciones subieron como la espuma* = My boss is in a good mood because his stocks shot through the roof. If you just can't seem to decide and are always wavering between good and bad moods, then you've probably earned the uncoveted and often feared title of *voluble* (moody).

Estar de ánimos = To be in the mood (spirits). More often than not, you will hear it spoken in the negative and it's usually because one is feeling down, sick, or tired. Patricia asks her friend Anabel to go out to lunch. If Anabel isn't in the mood, she might reply, *"No estoy de ánimos"* ("I'm not in the mood" or "I'm not in the spirit").

Antojarse means "to be in the mood for" or "to feel like" as it pertains to cravings and things one might fancy. *¿Qué se te antoja?* (What are you craving?) is what you would ask someone when deciding what to eat. If you're in the mood for a burger, then say, *"¿Sabes qué se me antoja? Se me antoja una hamburguesa"* ("You know what I'm in the mood for? I'm craving a burger"). If you're not in the mood for the fish-eyeball soup your brother suggested, then say, *"No se me antoja eso"* ("That doesn't appeal to me" or "It doesn't strike my fancy"). *Antojarse*, however, is not limited to the topic of food. It could be that you're in the mood for (or fancy) a movie or taking a walk in the park. *Se me antoja una película* = I feel like (or fancy) a movie. *Se me antoja un paseo por el parque* = I feel like (or fancy) a walk through the park.

Tener ganas de + the infinitive form of a verb = "To be in the mood for something" as it pertains to desires or urges. It can be an urge for anything in general: going out for sushi, going to the movies, or playing basketball, etc. You can see that it is very much like *antojarse*. *Tengo ganas de comer sushi* = I have a desire to eat sushi. *Tengo ganas de ir al cine* = I feel like going to the movies. When someone asks you to go fishing, for example, and the idea doesn't appeal to you, then you can respond with, *"No tengo ganas,"* which means that you are not in the mood.

Not get enough of, Not have one's fill

Some people just can't get enough. It's not necessarily a bad thing, nor does it necessarily mean that they're greedy (although they might be). In Spanish this is expressed as *no tener llena* (not to get enough of or not to have one's fill). When someone goes back for thirds, fourths, and even fifths at the buffet, one might snicker, *"Este muchacho no tiene llena"* ("This guy just can't get enough"). The same expression applies to any situation in which people can't get their fill of gossip, money, love, Spanish, and so on.

On the loose

Escaped criminals and stray dogs are examples of being "on the loose." In Spanish the verb is *andar suelto(a)*. On a scorching hot day, one could say, *"El diablo anda suelto"* for "The devil's on the loose." When disaster wreaks havoc such as during earthquakes, tornados, and fires, one could also say, *"El diablo anda suelto"* in the same way English speakers say, "All hell broke loose."

Overboard, Cross the line

Pasarse de la linea, pasarse de la raya, or just simply *pasarse* are the expressions in Spanish for "to go overboard," "to go too far," or "to cross the line." If, on your first date together, you catch your companion by surprise with a kiss and her reaction is less than receptive, then you could apologetically ask, *"¿Me pasé?"* ("Did I go too far?"). Let's say your wife is going way overboard and redefining the meaning of "cleaning house" by scrubbing every inch of the ceilings and walls of every room. You could tell her, *"No te pases de la raya limpiando la casa"* ("Don't go overboard cleaning the house").

Overshadow, Outdo, Outshine

The literal translation of the verb *opacar* is "to make opaque" or "less visible." Thus, it is quite logical how *opacar* came to be an excellent way of expressing "to overshadow," "outdo," or "outshine" in informal conversation. *María siempre opaca a su hermana por su belleza* = María always overshadows her sister with her beauty. *Cuando José canta en el coro de la escuela, opaca a todos los demás* = When José sings in the school choir, he overshadows all the rest.

Overwhelm, Wear out, Exhaust

For the native English speaker, learning Spanish can be quite a challenge. If you marry into a Spanish-speaking family from Mexico, as I did, then I have no doubt you were overwhelmed at family gatherings with everyone speaking to you at the same time at a decibel level equivalent to that of a rock concert. *Abrumar* and *agobiar* mean to overwhelm, wear out, or exhaust and are fitting words to describe this scenario. *Me siento muy abrumado* (or *agobiado*) *cuando toda la gente me habla a la misma vez* = I feel very overwhelmed (worn out, exhausted) when everyone talks to me at the same time. *No quiero abrumar* (or *agobiar*) *a la nueva empleada con tanto trabajo en su primer día* = I don't want to overwhelm (wear out, exhaust) the new employee with so much work on her first day.

Pamper

Mimar, consentir, and apapachar all mean to pamper, spoil, and dote on someone as a father might treat his little girl. *Martín mima todo el tiempo a su hija menor porque ella es muy curiosita* = Martín pampers his youngest daughter all the time because she's so cute.

Party

If you look at the agenda of most Gringos vacationing in a Spanish-speaking country, the top three "to do" items are probably party, party, and party. Well, since it's such a high priority item, I thought it fitting to include it in this book. After all, if you're going to spend so much time partying, you should at least know how to say it in the native language, right? To party in general (which typically includes alcohol, loud music, and dancing) is *pachanguear* or *ir de parranda*. *Vamos de parranda* = Let's party. A partier is called a *parrandero(a)*. *¡Qué parrandero(a) eres!* = You're such a partier! A bachelor(ette) party = *despedida de soltero(a)*. More civilized parties, like family get-togethers (assuming they are in fact civilized), are called *reuniones*. Last but not least, a birthday party can be referred to as a *cumpleaños, fiesta,* or *piñata* (for kids).

Pay attention

You may already be familiar with the phrases *poner atención* and *prestar atención* (to pay attention), but you must also become familiar with *hacer caso* (which is a cross between "to pay attention to" and "to listen to"). *Mi esposo no me hace caso* = My husband doesn't pay attention (listen) to me. *¡Hazme caso!* = Pay attention to me! or Listen to what I'm saying! The verb *fijarse* also means to pay attention but leans towards watching or listening closely or cautiously. *Fíjate bien, hijo* = Pay close attention, son. *Estos niños no se fijan cuando cruzan la calle* = These kids don't pay attention when they cross the street.

Pay the price

Pagar el pato = To "pay the price" for something or for someone else's mistake. Pay the duck, you're thinking? I don't know why it is, but it is. Before you start passing judgment, think about that expression "to pay the piper" and tell me if you know who this piper character is. What I do know is that this is quite a useful expression to convey how one person pays the price or consequences for something or for another's actions, shortcomings, mistakes, or faults. For example, let's suppose that you like things messy but your wife likes everything spic and span and therefore always picks up after you. *Tu esposa paga el pato por tu cochinero* = Your wife pays the price for your slobbiness. Let's look at another example: Every time your only daughter asks for something, you can't say no. Experienced parents might warn, *"Si consientes a tu hija, tú pagarás el pato después"* ("If you spoil your daughter, you'll pay for it later").

Plant things in someone's head

Calentar la cabeza literally means "to heat up the head," but in English this phrase is recognized as "to plant things in someone's head." This expression is often the source of many misunderstandings and heated arguments. It does not apply to benign ideas or thoughts like planting in your husband's head all of the wonderful things his mother-in-law has done so that he will get along with her. Rather, it is used to elicit quite the opposite effect. Suppose your long-lost sworn enemy resurfaces in your life one day and becomes buddies with your friend Diana. Suddenly Diana starts acting a little differently towards you, and you can tell something's fishy just by the "I never knew you were that kind of person" look in her eyes. Your first thought might be, *Le calentó la cabeza*, which means she (your sworn enemy) planted things in Diana's head.

Play dumb

Hacerse tonto(a), hacerse pato, and *hacerse pendejo(a)* are equally correct for "to play dumb." Take for example, Luz Waite and her three roommates conspicuously named Robin Yoo, Eaton Freely, and Ollie Caneat. Well, as roommates often do, they start having problems because all the food that Luz bought for the month (for herself) mysteriously disappears within a few days. Knowing that some or all of her roommates are responsible, Luz tells them, *"Díganme quién se comió toda mi comida y no se hagan tontos"* ("Tell me who ate all my food and don't play dumb"). To make life even easier, *hacerse tonto(a), hacerse pato,* and *hacerse pendejo(a)* can be shortened to *hacerse.* Thus, you will often hear the simpler *No te hagas* for "Don't play dumb."

Play hard to get

There she is again sitting alone at the other end of the café. Her name is Isabela and I've had my eye on her for a month. The first time I saw her at the café, she gave me her name but wouldn't let me buy her coffee. The second time, she let me buy her coffee but wouldn't accept a dinner invitation. The third time, we went out to dinner but she wouldn't go dancing afterwards. After a month of continuing with this charade, I finally had to tell her, *"¡Ay, Isabela, como te das a desear!"* ("Geez, Isabela, you sure play hard to get!") from the verb *darse a desear* (to play hard to get). On the opposite spectrum, you might also run across someone who will throw herself at your feet without a chase. *Perla no se da a desear porque sale con cualquier muchacho que apenas acaba de conocer* = Perla doesn't play hard to get because she goes out with any guy that she just met.

Play it cool, Act cool

You're talking to your wife on a cell phone in a crowded bus and the normally soft, sweet voice that you use in private suddenly turns deep and macho in public. Since your wife knows you better, she would tell you, *"No te pases de listo en frente de toda la gente"* ("Don't try and act all cool in front of everyone"). In this example, *pasarse de listo* means "to play it cool" or "to act cool," but it also has a secondary meaning. For that, see "Pull a fast one."

Pull a fast one

We already learned from the previous entry that *pasarse de listo* means to act cool (see "Play it cool," "Act cool"). *Pasarse de listo(a)*, however, also means to be slick or sly enough to "pull a fast one" on someone. Suppose you and your wife are at a restaurant eating the most delicious steak. You notice she's almost done with her meal but you still have plenty to go. You turn your head to look for the waiter to ask for more water and when you look back, you notice that your wife has switched plates. You point to her and say, *"Te pasaste de lista. Me cambiaste los platos"* ("You're really slick. You switched plates"). In this context, it is usually spoken with an accusing but lighthearted tone. Here's another example: You're looking to buy a shirt at a cash-only shop. The salesperson tells you that the shirt costs twenty dollars and so you buy it. Later, you discover that the shirt actually costs ten dollars, and that the salesperson pocketed the extra ten dollars. *"El vendedor se pasó de listo con nosotros,"* you whisper to your friend ("The salesman pulled a fast one on us").

Put on one's game face

In English we say, "I'm going to put on my game face" or "I'm going to get serious" when we need to perform at our absolute best, or when the task at hand will take one's complete concentration and it's time to stop messing around and time to get serious. In Spanish one might hear *ponerse trucha* to convey this same idea. Why *trucha*? *Trucha* means trout, doesn't it? Of course it does, and it's because trout can snag that bait off the hook as soon as it hits the water. In other words, trout are quick and smart. They don't mess around or second-guess things or else they will miss their meal. Follow this example. Alonsito was lying down with a video game joystick in hand, just cruising through stages one, two, and three of his game. When he reached level four (the most difficult level), it was do or die. *"Ahora voy a ponerme trucha"* ("Now I'm gonna get serious"), he said as he got up off his belly to devote his full attention to the game. In the same way Alonsito devotes his attention to his video game, the same could be said about doing one's schoolwork. For example, Alonsito's mother might tell him, *"Ponte trucha en la escuela para que aprendas rápido"* ("Be prepared and buckle down at school so that you learn fast").

Put someone on the spot (spotlight)
To be between a rock and a hard place

You're sound asleep in class when your teacher asks the class a question. Your "friend" puts you on the spot by volunteering you to answer. Now all eyes are on you. *Te puso entre la espada y la pared* (He put you "on the spot," "in the spotlight," or "between a rock and a hard place") from the expression *poner alguien entre la espada y la pared* (to put someone on the spot). The literal translation is "to put someone between the sword and the wall." Spoken with the verb *estar* (*estar entre la espada y la pared*), this phrase can also be said when having to make a tough decision between equally good (or bad) choices. *Estoy entre la espada y la pared porque los dos trabajos que me ofrecieron son buenos* = I'm stuck between a rock and a hard place because both jobs they offered me are good.

Put someone to the test

Poner alguien a prueba = To put someone to the test, to test someone. When asked if you speak Spanish, you could respond, *"Sí, pero no me pongas a prueba"* ("Yes, but don't put me to the test"). The same expression can be used by angry parents warning their unruly kids not to test their patience. *Niños, no me pongan a prueba* = Kids, don't test me.

Rat on someone, Tattle, Squeal

Delatar = To tattle, squeal, or rat on someone. After sneaking cookies past my parents' bedroom and into my bed late at night, I would tell my little sister, *"No me delates o me van a castigar"* ("Don't tattle on me or they're going to punish me").

Refresh one's memory

Refrescar la memoria is to refresh one's memory. This is something your significant other might do around Christmas, birthdays, or anniversaries. After asking her why she deserves that diamond-studded bracelet, she tells you, *"Déjame refrescar tu memoria"* ("Allow me to refresh your memory") as she reminds you of all the wonderful things she has done for you. For almost any situation in which you don't recall something, you can say, *"Refréscame la memoria"* ("Refresh my memory").

Regret

Arrepentirse = To regret something. It's not the easiest word to pronounce, but practice makes perfect. Learn it or else *te vas a arrepentir* (You'll regret it). *Si no estudias español, te arrepentirás después* = If you don't study Spanish, you'll regret it later. The noun for regret is *remordimiento. No tengo ningún remordimiento* = I don't regret anything.

Rely on

There are a few ways to express the verb "to rely on." The first is for people who can be relied on (*contar con*). *Siempre puedo contar con mi esposa cuando tengo problemas* = I can always count on my wife when I have problems. Then there are those who can't seem to do anything without relying on other people (*atenerse*). It can be as innocent as an infant who relies entirely on her parents or as annoying as someone who is just plain lazy. *Roberto es muy flojo y siempre se atiene a otra gente para todo* = Roberto is very lazy and always relies on other people for everything. To describe people who purposely and selfishly take advantage of other people, use *colgarse* (see "Take advantage of" later in this chapter).

Reputation

Some people guard their reputations with their lives, while others really could care less what people think of them. Once you get a reputation, however, it's often hard to shake. *Tener fama* (literally, "to have fame") = To have a reputation. *Mi amiga Marcia tiene fama de ser irresponsable* = My friend Marcia has the reputation of being irresponsible. Keep in mind that *tener fama* can also be said for positive reputations like the neighborhood *taquería* famous for making the best Mexican food west of the Mississippi. If you develop an unfavorable reputation that you just can't shed, then *estás quemado(a)* (you're burned up). It is another way of saying that you've proven way too many times that you can't be counted on for whatever task is at hand. For example, Roberto offers to organize Ignacio's bachelor party. Judging from Roberto's shaky past record, however, it is an absolute certainty that he won't follow through with his word, and everyone knows it. So Ignacio may appoint someone else to take charge because *Roberto está quemado.*

Rip off, Swindle, Overcharge

Both *estafar* and *cargar la mano* mean to rip off, swindle, or overcharge someone. You may have noticed that many countries have tourist souvenir shops that don't have price tags on the merchandise, and yes, it is often because there are two prices: one for those who speak the native language and one for those who don't (and don't have the confidence to bargain or simply don't know any better). No need to ask who pays the higher price. *Me estafaron porque sabían que yo era turista* = They ripped me off because they knew that I was a tourist. As a word of caution, be careful not to use these terms in front of the vendors, as these words carry heavy accusations. Remember, bargaining is part of the game in many parts of the world. Learn the game and you won't have to risk offending anyone. In the example above, one can also use *cargar la mano* (literally, "to charge the hand") instead of the verb *estafar*. *Cargar la mano,* however, is much like the expression *sacar el jugo*. See "Squeeze or milk what you can get" later in this chapter. These expressions describe how your slavedriver boss treats you, for example. *Mi jefe siempre me carga la mano con el trabajo de la oficina* = My boss always overworks me in the office. In this sentence, the use of *cargar la mano* implies that your boss is getting more out of you than he's paying for.

If you want to explain how someone "swindled" you or "pulled the wool over your eyes" by selling you "shit for shoe polish" (excuse the expression), use *dar gato por liebre* (literally, "to give a cat for a hare"). If you paid the jeweler for a "twenty-four-karat" gold necklace that turned green in the shower, then you can say, *"Me dio gato por liebre"* or *"Me vendió gato por liebre,"* which is to say, "He swindled me," "He pulled the wool over my eyes," "He sold me shit for shoe polish," or the like.

Risk it all, Go for broke

Jugarse el todo por el todo = To risk it all, go for broke. You've just hit a lucky streak at the blackjack table and now you have $15,000 in casino chips stacked neatly in front of you. If you double your winnings, you can buy that $30,000 car you've been dreaming about. Your luck has been so good that you decide to risk it all and "go for broke." In other words, you want to bet "all or nothing" on the next hand. *"Me juego el todo por el todo"* ("I'm going for it all"), you tell the dealer as you push all your chips into the betting circle.

Root for

¿A quién le vas? You will often hear this phrase before a sporting event. It means "Who are you rooting for?" Keep in mind that the indirect object pronoun *le* never changes regardless of who is speaking to whom. Only the verb *ir* is conjugated according to who the subject is. *Le voy a México* = I'm voting for Mexico. *Le van a Corea del Sur* = They're voting for South Korea. *Le va a Alemania* = She's voting for Germany.

Rub it in someone's face

In English we "rub it in the face" or "rub salt in the wounds" when we want to gloat over our own triumphs or someone else's defeat or misfortune. In Spanish the term is *restregar en la cara*. You just lost a hundred-dollar bet with your friend because your team lost to his team in the championship game. The next day he hangs the sports page on your door so that you can't miss it. The more cynical example would be the classmate who sees that you received a failing grade on your term paper and so "accidentally" drops his A+ paper at your feet for you to pick up for him. Perhaps the most diabolical illustration would be your ex-girlfriend stealing away your best friend and making it a point to walk hand in hand by your window every day. In each painful example, *te lo están restregando en la cara* (They're rubbing it in your face). Barring obscenities, you can remark, *"¡Sí, sí, restriégamelo en mi cara!"* to say, "Yeah, yeah, rub it in my face, why don't you!" *No lo restriegues en mi cara* = Don't rub it in (my face).

Rummage through someone's things

Esculcar = To rummage through something. Usually reserved for those who stick their paws where they don't belong. A hungry cat might do this in your garbage and a suspicious boyfriend might do this to your purse. Believe it or not, I've also seen nosy people walk into my home and actually go through my mail. If this happens to you, tell them, *"¡No esculques mis cosas, metiche!"* ("Don't be going through my things, nosy!").

Sensitive

Sentirse = To be sensitive (feelings easily affected). Suppose your sister asks you what your true opinion is about her boyfriend. Before telling her what you really think about the cocky bastard, you might want to forewarn her by saying, *"No te sientas"* ("Don't get sensitive"). *Se siente mucho cuando lo critico* = He gets very sensitive when I criticize him. *Agüitarse* is a very common verb that closely resembles the definition of *sentirse,* but bear in mind that these two words are distinctly different in meaning. You will likely encounter *agüitarse* frequently in conversation, so it will serve you well to know the distinction between the two. *Agüitarse* means to get down or depressed (but not necessarily sensitive). You can say, *"No te agüites"* ("Don't lose hope") to your friend who is having a difficult time finding a job, or to your wife who was unable to spend Christmas with her family in Mexico, for example.

Set someone up

Your best friend, Derek, is single and a perfect match for your coworker Gloria, so you decide to set them up. *Voy a encasquetar a Derek con Gloria* = I'm going to set up Derek with Gloria. It is important to note that the verb *encasquetar* is used when one sets up *other* people, and the ones getting set up have no say in the matter, such as in the above example. If individuals want to set themselves up, then use *ligar* or *tirar la onda* (see "Flirt" earlier in this chapter). *Encasquetar* can also be said for leaving someone responsible for someone or something in much the same manner that the verb *encargar* (to put in charge, to make responsible for) is used. *Este cabrón me encasquetó a su hermano mientras se fue de compras* = This jerk left me in charge of his brother while he went shopping.

Show off

Pararse el cuello = To show off or act cool. Literally, it means "to stand the collar up," which makes sense if you think about it. Let's say you're at a disco with your buddies and your group ends up hooking up with a group of gals. At the end of the night, the bill arrives and your otherwise penny-pinching friend, Juan, uncharacteristically grabs it and pays for everyone. *"Mira como Juan se para el cuello para apantallar a las muchachas,"* you whisper to the other guys. It means "Check out how Juan is showing off to impress the women." (Also, see "Play it cool" earlier in this chapter.)

Show your true colors

Enseñar el cobre and *sacar el cobre* = To show one's true colors. Literally, it means to "show the copper" perhaps referring to one's true persona underneath the gold-plated exterior. *Elena enseño el cobre* (or *sacó el cobre*) *cuando eructó en la mesa* = Elena showed her true colors when she burped at the table.

Shower with attention

Hacer tanta fiesta (literally, "to make a big party") = To shower someone with attention (or praise). It actually means that someone is overdoing it and giving too much praise or attention to someone. An example of this would be the outcast trying to fit in with the popular crowd. He or she may worship and praise everything the crowd does. Another example is the husband who kisses and hugs his wife for every little cute thing that she does. The receiver of all this attention can say, *"¡No me hagas tanta fiesta!"* which translates to "Stop overdoing it with all this attention!"

Shut someone up

Callar is the verb in Spanish to express "shutting someone up." Naturally, it means to make someone stop talking, mumbling, singing, or making noise. *Te callé* = I shut you up. We've all heard *¡Cállate!* (Shut up!) from the verb *callarse*. *María estaba cotorreando toda la noche y no se callaba* = María was babbling all night long and wouldn't shut up. Whenever in doubt, you can revert to the always reliable Shhhhhh! We can also shut someone up or deflate someone's big head and even bigger ego by "putting the person in his or her place" with the expression *poner alguien en su lugar* (to put someone in his or her place) or by "shutting him or her up" with *tapar la boca* (to shut the mouth). *Pablo siempre me presumía que es buen jugador de baloncesto, pero lo puse en su lugar* (or *le tapé la boca*) *cuando jugué en contra de él* = Pablo always bragged to me that he is a good basketball player, but I put him in his place (or "shut him up") when I played against him.

Tirar a salir is to shut someone up in quite a different way. It would be the equivalent of throwing a dog a bone just to shut him up and get him off your back. For example, your wife is going on and on about what outfit she should wear to the dinner party and then she asks for your opinion. You don't really care too much about the subject and you may even be a little preoccupied watching your favorite show on television. So, half-enthusiastically and perhaps not so convincingly, you say, "Yeah, … that would be great," with the hopes that it would be a satisfactory answer to keep her quiet. Because she's a lot smarter than you give her credit for, she then responds with an angry, "*¡No más tiras a salir!*" A close translation would be something like "You're throwing anything out there just to shut me up."

Sick of, Fed up

Estar harto(a) de means "to be sick of" or "fed up with" anything (people, food, etc.). *Estoy harto del caldo de pollo porque lo he comido cuatro días seguidos* = I'm sick of chicken broth because I have eaten it for the last four days. When it is already understood that you're sick of something, then say, "*Me tiene harto(a)*" for "I'm sick of it." For most purposes it's the better and easier choice. Several steps beyond *estar harto(a) de* or *odiar* (to hate), *aborrecer* takes it to a new level. It is used when you are completely sick of or disgusted with someone or something to the point where just the thought of it (whatever "it" may be) would make you vomit. For example, your neighbor asks you if you want a shot of tequila. After drinking way too much tequila for the past month you reply, "*Tengo aborrecido el tequila porque tomé como loco el mes pasado*" ("I'm completely sick of tequila because I drank it like crazy the past month"). Just as a side note, I want to mention that practically every dictionary states that the word *tequila* takes the feminine article *la*. I have yet to come across a native speaker of Spanish, however, who agrees with the dictionary. In fact, the native speakers with whom I have consulted, vehemently insist that the article for *tequila* takes the masculine *el*, and that if the dictionary states *la*, the dictionary is wrong.

Spaced out, Out of it

There are some people who just can't keep their lights on, and it's not because they are conserving energy. A conversation between you and a woman like this soon ends up being you talking to yourself, and the other person staring into space—a place the person may even call home. She's not sleeping. In fact, her eyes are wide open but she's staring at the wall as if she's never seen one before. This phenomenon of "spacing out" is expressed in Spanish by *estar ido(a)*, which translates more literally as "to be gone." *Ella está muy ida. He estado platicando con ella y se queda viendo a la pared.* = She's so out of it (spaced out). I've been chatting with her and she keeps staring at the wall.

Split, Go halves with

Ir por mitad = To go halves with someone. It is normally associated with splitting something like the restaurant bill or the cost of a taxi fare, for example. *Los precios en este restaurante están caros, así que vamos por mitad* = The prices at this restaurant are high, so let's split the bill. *Compartir* (to share) or *dividir* (to divide) are equally effective ways of conveying the same. *Compartimos la cuenta* = Let's split the bill. One could also say, *"Compartimos mitad-mitad"* for "Let's split half-and-half" or "Let's split fifty-fifty." Even an abbreviated *mitad-mitad* will do.

Spread rumors

More contagious than chicken pox and more rampant than a herd of stampeding buffalo, rumors about other people can overrun an office faster than a speeding bullet. *Correr el rumor* = To spread rumors. *Corre el rumor de que Antonio está teniendo una relación extramarital con Juana* = Rumor is spreading that Antonio is having an extramarital affair with Juana.

Squeeze or milk what you can get
(in order to take full advantage)

Sacar el jugo literally means to "extract the juice." Figuratively, it means "to milk" or "squeeze" every drop one can get or "to get one's money's worth." Undoubtedly, we've all heard of companies that run more like boot camps than offices and that work their people more like horses than human beings. The employees of these labor factories might complain, *"En esta compañía les sacan el jugo a sus trabajadores"* ("In this company they squeeze every drop out of their workers"). Here's another example. You and your wife just arrived at your company party and there are plenty of delicious all-you-can-eat appetizers and free-flowing drinks for everyone. Before you can take advantage of them, however, your wife says you both have to leave because she's worried about the kids at home. You tell her, *"Ya que estamos aquí, ¿por qué no le sacamos el jugo?"* ("Since we're here now, why don't we take full advantage?").

Stick out, Stand out

What do the seven-foot jockey, the four-foot center of the basketball team, and the three-hundred-pound gymnast have in common? The answer is that they stand out, stick out, jump at you, and take your attention. In Spanish you can take your pick with the verbs *resaltar*, *sobresalir,* or *destacar* to express these notions. *A Carlos le gusta sobresalir de los demás y por eso siempre se viste con ropa carísima y a la última moda* = Carlos likes to stand out from others, and that's why he always dresses in expensive, fashionable clothing.

Stop by, Pass through, Go in and out

You and your family are on hour five of a ten-hour drive back home from vacation when your wife spots the jewelry outlet store that she's always wanted to check out. Everybody else in the car just wants to go straight home, but it's your wife's only chance. So she pleads, *"No más vamos de pasadita"* (from *ir de pasadita*), which means "Let's just pass by real quick" or "Let's just stop by for a second." Similarly, *Vamos de entrada por salida* (from *ir de entrada por salida*) is a good way to express the same thing. It means "We'll just go in and out real quick."

Street smarts

Tener colmillo = To have street smarts. Literally, this means "to have fang." The word *colmillo* refers to our two canines (the two sharp teeth on the upper corners of your smile). Why *colmillo*? To be street smart, you naturally have to be sharper than the rest and, like Dracula, you're the one who takes the bite out of other people, not the other way around. *Para vivir en este peligroso barrio, tienes que tener colmillo o no sobrevives* = To live in this rough neighborhood, you have to have street smarts or you won't survive.

Stretch your resources (time, money, etc.)

Rendir is the verb you need to use to express how you might "stretch" your resources. Essentially, it means to "stretch" or "get the most out of" something and usually refers to either time or money. Suppose you're in a little town called *Pueblo Barato* (Cheap Town) and there you can buy a gallon of milk for what amounts to about twenty-five cents in U.S. dollars. *"Aquí el dinero rinde,"* you might say ("Here our money goes a long way"). Don't use *rendir* when you want to express stretching your legs. The correct verb for that is *estirar*.

Stuffed

Estar retacado(a) = To be stuffed. A file cabinet that is filled to the last inch is *retacado*. In addition, this can also be said about how "stuffed" we may feel after eating a forty-ounce steak. One could say the usual, *"Estoy lleno"* ("I'm full"), but if you want to impress someone with your Spanish prowess, then say, *"Estoy retacado."* For added emphasis and a little humor, stick *hasta la coronilla* at the end (I'm stuffed up to the crown of my head). Okay, it may not sound so humorous to you, but put it to the test and you'll see.

Surround oneself with

The old saying goes, "Tell me who your friends are and I'll tell you who you are." In Spanish the phrase is, *Dime con quién andas y te diré quién eres.* So with whom do you surround yourself? To answer that question, use *rodearse de* (to surround oneself with). *Él siempre se rodea de mujeres bellas* = He always surrounds himself with beautiful women.

Take advantage of

In Spanish *tomar ventaja de, aprovecharse*, and *colgarse* mean "to take advantage of"—*colgarse* being the most drastic of the three. *Tomar ventaja* and *aprovecharse* don't necessarily imply that you are imposing upon anyone. It could be that you're taking advantage of a golden opportunity for a promotion at work or a much needed vacation without the kids. The verb *colgarse*, however, implies a direct encroachment on other people. You should think twice before lending a helping hand to a couple described as *colgados(as)* because you might regret it. You offer to babysit their kids for one night and pretty soon you might as well call them your kids. *No les quiero dar la mano porque siempre se cuelgan de nosotros* = I don't want to give them a hand because they always take advantage of us.

Take back what one says

Retirar lo dicho = To take back what one says. Everyone says things they wish they hadn't, so learning this expression will serve you well one day. It is pretty much the same as saying, "I spoke too soon." In calculus your fellow classmate asks how you're doing on your exams. As you reply how easy the tests are, your professor drops your latest exam on your desk, and written on the front is a big, fat red-letter "F." You then turn to your classmate and say, *"Retiro lo dicho"* for "I spoke too soon" or "I take that back."

Take credit for something someone else did

If you can learn this phrase, I tip my hat to you because it sounds impressive even when a native Spanish speaker says it. *Hacer caravana con sombrero ajeno* means to take credit for something someone else did. Literally, it means to tip one's hat from afar. Allow me to illustrate. You're throwing a huge birthday party for your brother. You've already done all of the legwork single-handedly and everything is set. On the day of the party when all the guests arrive, your brother's girlfriend suddenly takes charge as if she were the one who arranged the whole thing from the beginning. *Ella está tratando de hacer caravana con sombrero ajeno* = She's trying to take credit for someone else's work. Of course if you prefer things simple, use *tomar crédito* instead.

Take sides

Ponerse de parte de = To take sides. *Parece que Natalia es la consentida de la familia porque nuestros padres siempre se ponen de parte de ella* = It seems like Natalia is the favorite in the family because our parents always take her side.

Tease

Dar carrilla or *burlarse de* = To tease. It's not the kind of "tease" a hairdresser might do to someone's hair, but you can certainly tease someone about his or her hair if you think it looks funny. *Toda la clase le está dando carrilla a Daniel por su nuevo corte de pelo* = Everyone in class is teasing Daniel because of his new haircut. *No te burles de mi* = Don't make fun of me. Keep in mind that *dar carrilla* is spoken informally among friends and family and *burlarse de* is spoken in the presence of more formal company.

Test the waters

Tantear el punto = To test the waters. It means to gauge the mood or "atmosphere" before deciding to do something. Let's say you need to ask Dad for one hundred dollars, knowing full well that he's already in a bad mood. You decide to ask anyway but before doing so, *tanteas el punto para ver cuál es el mejor momento para pedir el dinero* (You test the waters to see the most opportune moment to ask for the money).

Thick-skinned

Pay close attention to this one because it is a very useful expression. However, the definition in Spanish covers more ground than its English counterpart. *Hacer concha* = To be thick-skinned, callous, or hardened. The literal meaning is "to make a shell" like a snail who hides under its protective shell cover whenever it feels threatened. In English we tend to use the word thick-skinned to mean someone who is unaffected by criticism or emotion, or who is sometimes insensitive. The same is true in Spanish. One step further, however, the Spanish definition also means to be so thick-skinned, unphased, and unaffected as "not to lift a finger" and "not to give a damn" about it even if one should. Suppose a group of volunteers has gathered to help out the local community. There is one volunteer, however, lounging on the chair talking to his friend on his cell phone all day while everyone else is working hard. The rest of the group is probably all thinking the same thing, *¡Mira como hace concha este muchacho!* A good translation of this would be "Look how this guy is so comfortable and doesn't even lift a finger."

Think too highly of oneself

While touring the party circuit in Mexico, I quickly became familiar with this expression as friendly locals would point out who all the snobs were among the crowd. To think too highly of oneself is *creerse*. *Se cree mucho* is the general phrase for "He's full of himself" or "She thinks the world of herself." If you want to be more specific, just add the appropriate adjective at the end. *Se cree cremosa* = She thinks she's so high-class. *Se cree guapo* = He thinks he's so handsome.

Throw a pitch (sales pitch)

Every good salesperson has a "pitch" he or she uses in order to bait you into buying a certain product or idea. Like the baseball term "to pitch," the word in Spanish is *pichar*. This term is what many would call "Spanglish" or a *pochismo*, meaning that the word is a hybrid of English and Spanish. On deciding where to eat for dinner, your wife may ask, "*¿Qué me vas a pichar?*" What she's basically asking you is, "What's your proposal?" or "What's the best you can come up with?" The verb *disparar* (to shoot) is an equally common alternative. *¿Qué me vas a disparar?* and *¿Qué me vas a pichar?* mean the same thing.

Ton

There will be times when the adjective *mucho* (a lot) is just not the word you're looking for when referring to large quantities or amounts of something. For example, you might say, "There are a lot of things on sale at the store" when you really want to say, "There is a ton of things on sale at the store." *Chorro*, *montón*, and *chingo* are the adjectives that come into play here (note: *chingo* is a crude Mexican term). *Había un montón de cosas en oferta en la tienda* = There was a ton of things on sale at the store. A ton (2,204.62 lbs.) in Spanish is actually *una tonelada*, but if you were to use *tonelada* in this example, one might think that there was literally one ton's worth (2,204.62 lbs.) of merchandise on sale at the store (As a reminder, see the sixth entry under "Troubleshooting" in chapter 2, under "Do-It-Yourself Spanish").

Turn someone on, Turn someone off

In Spanish there are several verbs that express turning someone on or off. The verbs *prender* and *encender* mean "to turn on," and they can be either sexual or nonsexual. The verbs *apagar, desanimar,* and *desilusionar* mean "to turn off." Of these three, only *apagar* can be sexual. *Me apagas cuando dices malas palabras* = You turn me off when you say bad words. Perhaps this is not the best example, as undoubtedly there are those people who are actually turned on by the same dirty words. You get the point.

Turn the table

Voltear la tortilla or *referir* = To turn the table. Your father is lecturing you about the dangers of drinking too much alcohol. You strike first with a defiant, "*¿Y tú? ¡Tomabas mucho cuando eras joven también!*" ("And what about you? You drank a lot when you were young, too!"). Your father then counterpunches and says, "*¡No me voltees la tortilla!*" (or "*¡No me refieras!*"). That is to say, "Don't turn the tables!" or "Don't make this about me!"

Understand, Get it

During the course of a conversation it is important to know that the person you're speaking to understands what you're saying or you'd just be wasting precious oxygen. There are several ways to find out. The always reliable *¿Me entiendes?* (Do you understand me?) and *¿Me explico?* (Do I make sense?) are usually the first choices. *Caer el veinte* is more colloquial and can sound a little disparaging if taken the wrong way. Literally, it means, "to fall the twenty," perhaps referring to a twenty-piece coin being dropped through the slot in order to get the electricity flowing. It is used when you expect someone to understand something that he or she doesn't quite get, like a joke or an explanation of how to solve a math problem, for example. "*¡Por fin te cayó el veinte!*" ("You finally got it!"), you say to your little brother who finally got the joke. *Captar* means "to grasp" or "to get" an idea or concept. "*¿Captas?*" ("Got it?"), you ask your cousin. "*Sí, pero no capté al principio,*" or "*Sí, pero no me cayó el veinte al principio*" ("Yes, but I didn't get it at first"), she replies back.

The versatile *agarrar* provides us with several good alternatives. Suppose you walk in on your wife and mother's gossip session, which suspiciously simmers down to a whisper as soon as you enter the room. Unfortunately for them, it was too late because even with just hearing a few key words, you knew they were talking about the time you wet your pants on the roller-coaster. "*¡Lo agarraste en el aire!*" ("You got the drift!" or "You pieced it together!"), your wife admits. This comes from the expression *agarrar en el aire*, which literally means "to catch in the air." In other words, you didn't have to hear the entire conversation because you already had put two and two together. *Agarrar la onda* or just *agarrar* are both good fits for "to get it," "to get the picture," and "to get the hint." Remember the Víctor and Selena example from the entry "Hint" earlier in this chapter? Well, feeding off of that example, *A pesar de todas las indirectas que Selena le dio a Víctor, él no agarró la onda* = In spite of all of the hints that Selena gave Víctor, he didn't get it.

Up to one's old tricks

Hacer de las suyas = To be up to one's old tricks or old ways. Fernando was supposedly a changed man and was no longer getting into trouble, but when I saw him hanging out with the neighborhood thugs again, I thought to myself, *Allí va otra vez, haciendo de las suyas* (There he goes again, up to his old ways).

Up to something, On the move

Traer movida means "to be up to something suspicious," "to be on the move," "to cook up something," or "to plan something sneaky." An example of this would be your sister, who one Saturday night suddenly starts using make-up for the first time and puts on a nice dress with fancy high heels. Knowing that T-shirts and jeans are all that she ever wears, you say suspiciously, "*¡Traes movida!*" You can also say, "*Traes alguna movida.*" Both translate to "You're up to something," "You're on the move," or "What have you got up your sleeve?"

Walking on clouds

In English we say that people are "in the clouds" or "on cloud nine" when they're hopelessly in love, when they've just won the state lottery, or when they're just so excited about something that they can't get their minds off it. In Spanish *andar volado(a)* (to be in flight) and *estar en las nubes* (to be in the clouds) are the verbal expressions used to convey this. You can say, *"Andas volado"* to your cousin Beto who's at the café with friends but is not saying a word. He's just sitting there with a big smile on his face and a slight blush, thinking about the fantastic gal he just met. Now let's suppose your friend Linda just bought a new shiny red convertible. Since she can't take her eyes off the car and can't wait to take all of her friends out for a spin, you tell her, *"Andas volada con el carro nuevo."* Note: In some countries, *volado(a)* means "high" from smoking pot, for example.

Now, if your dreamer friend tells you that she's going to open a restaurant chain across the country, buy a multimillion-dollar house, and then fly around the world on a moment's notice, then the slightly more down-to-earth phrases *andar volado(a)* and *estar en las nubes* don't apply. For this example, tell your friend, *"Estás haciendo castillos en el aire"* ("You're making castles in the air").

Walking on thin ice, On the bubble

To be walking on thin ice or "on the bubble" can be expressed with *estar en la cuerda floja* (literally, "to be on a loose rope"), which, oddly enough, translates as "to be on a tightrope" in English. *José está en la cuerda floja y si no se apura, reprobará el año* = José is walking on thin ice (on the bubble) and if he doesn't speed up, he'll flunk out.

Weasel, Snooker

Encandilar = To "weasel" or "snooker" someone into doing something. Generally speaking, it means to convince or take advantage of someone by luring, baiting, or tricking the person into something oftentimes by impressing or wowing them. You're on vacation and strolling through the hotel lobby when an attractive and young woman approaches and offers you free tours, show tickets, and dinner if you just come and take a quick look at a time-share presentation. Of course, she assures you that you are under no obligation whatsoever. Well, once you're in the presentation, the high-pressure tactics kick in, and four hours later, you walk away owning a time-share you really didn't want. *No quería comprar el tiempo compartido, pero me encandilaron* = I didn't want to buy the time-share but they snookered me into it. Since the literal definition of *encandilar* is "to dazzle" or "put someone in a daze," it should be noted that this verb is said when referring to magicians who mesmerize an audience with their magic. It can also be used when you are blinded by the bright light from the idiot driving behind you with his high beams on, for example.

Work oneself to death

There are some people who just can't rest even when their work is finished. Workaholics fall into this category. Let's say, for example, that your friend just flew in from across the globe to visit you. As soon as you both arrive back to your place, he can't find a minute to relax. Instead, he wants to take everything out of his four suitcases, reorganize and hang up all of his clothes, clean and set up his room, clean the kitchen, cook something to eat, and then … well, you get the picture. *"No te tires a matar,"* you can tell him. This essentially means "Don't work yourself to death" from the expression *tirarse a matar*. In this same example, you can even use the verb *matarse* (literally, "to kill oneself") instead of *tirarse a matar* and the meaning would not change. *¡No te mates tanto!* = Don't overwork yourself!

Tirarse a matar is also a good expression for going "full-bore" or "all-out" (some may even choose the crude expression "balls out") when engaging in an activity with no regard for the potential hazard or injury that may result. One might comment, *"¡Mira como se tiran a matar!"* about two teams relentlessly battling each other in the Super Bowl. Another example would be children who might recklessly throw themselves off the couch and run around at full speed, slamming into walls and stepping on anything that gets in their way.

6

Watching Your Language

The Essentials of
Madre, Chingar, Cabrón(a), and *Pendejo(a)*

Let's face it. Curse words, swear terms, and other lesser-refined vocabulary, called *groserías*, have infiltrated nearly every known language. The truth is that *groserías* are also an important part of the Spanish language, and like it or not, they have become an integral part of everyday conversation in Spanish. I dare say these are terms we should definitely know and become familiar with unless we choose to limit our ability to fully comprehend conversations with native speakers. No offense is intended—it is simply how people talk. I'm not saying you should actually use these words on other people, but in the appropriate company, why not put a few curse words into practice? Don't forget the name of this book— *Speaking Spanish Like a Native.* Believe me, it is only to your advantage to be able to understand these words when you hear them spoken, and you will likely hear them spoken frequently.

Furthermore, I believe that there are few better ways to express the intensity of your emotions or opinions than with the use of *groserías.* Imagine trying to express to your friend the anger you felt during a heated argument with your neighbor, or the frustration you felt with an annoying coworker, but without using a single *grosería.* It's hard to imagine, isn't it? Undoubtedly, many of you have this ability to refrain from using foul language, but believe me when I tell you that a great many of the people with whom you will converse, in any language, do not have the same self-control. We simply need these words to blow off steam and to accentuate our emotions. With that said, we'll concentrate on the big four: *Madre, Chingar, Cabrón,* and *Pendejo.*

Madre

Madre, as you may already know, means "mother." In most cultures, the mother holds the most revered place in the family, and this holds true without exception in the Latino family (just don't tell Dad). So respected is the mother, in fact, that to use her name in vain is one of the best ways to let people know you mean business; thus, *madre* has been chosen as "the mother of all things" irreverent and disrespectful.

Un desmadre is a big mess or ruckus, like a crowd of rowdy kids screaming outside your window, but it can also refer to your filthy, unkempt room, for example. *Un madrazo* is a "hit" or "blow" (not drug related). *Le puse un madrazo a mi amigo* = I hit my friend. The expression *¡Pura madre!* is a crude and slightly resigned way of saying, "What the hell" or "Oh, well, whatever!" When something doesn't go your way, you can say this while throwing your hands in the air.

Un(a) valemadrista is someone who just doesn't give a damn. The *valemadrista* will be rude without remorse and will do as he or she damn well pleases without consideration of others. Criticizing his or her lack of tact or sensitivity will fall on deaf ears because this type just doesn't give a damn. Naturally, that leads us to *no tener madre*, which means "not to give a damn"—something the shameless *valemadrista* does very well. *Fabián no tiene madre* literally means that Fabián doesn't have a mother. This very well may be true, but in the world of *groserías*, it means that Fabián doesn't give a rat's ass. *Valer madre* is just another way of saying the same thing, and of course, the *valemadrista* no doubt makes good use of both of these verbs. *Me vale madre* = I don't give a damn! *Le vale madre* means that he or she doesn't give a damn. *¡Vale madre!* all by itself (without the indirect-object pronoun) means "It sucks!" or "It ain't worth shit!" You can say this about anything that hasn't met your expectations like that new cell phone that never gets clear reception, for example.

¡Tu madre! is a classic smart-ass remark that translates to "Your mama!" *¡Ni madre!* means "No way!" or "Like hell!" Your overprotective older brother tells you he's going to accompany you and your date to your prom. *"¡Ni madre!"* you tell him. *Cagar la madre* means "to piss the shit out of someone," but should only be reserved for especially maddening occasions. It is quite a harsh expression, so try not to use it when it's not necessary.

Me caga la madre cuando le presto cosas a Miguel y no me las devuelve = It pisses the shit out of me when I lend things to Miguel and he doesn't return them.

A toda madre is the exception to all this mother-bashing. It means "totally cool" or "awesome." When used with the verb *ser*, it refers to cool people. *Eres a toda madre* = You're awesome. When used with the verb *estar*, it refers to cool things. For example, if your neighbor just bought a sleek, shiny red sports car, you can say, "*¡Está a toda madre!*" for "It's totally cool!" This more flattering usage of *madre* is similar to how the term *padre* is used. For some reason, *padre* has been chosen to represent things that are cool as they pertain to things but not people. *¡Tú carro nuevo está muy padre!* = Your new car is totally cool!

Madre also gives us one of the snappier answers that Spanish has to offer. By sticking the word *madre* after a conjugated verb, you have changed the meaning of the verb to mean just the opposite but with a little sarcastic punch. Let me explain: *Voy* means "I'm going." *Voy madre* means "There's no way in hell that I'm going." If your brother volunteers you to run to the market to buy snacks by telling you, "*Vete al mercado para comprar botanas*" ("Go to the market to buy snacks"), then you could reply, "*Voy madre*" for "Like hell I'm going!" or "Go to the store my ass!"

Chingar

Chingar is another mainstay in the diet of daily Spanish conversation and I'll bet that even if you know only a handful of words in Spanish, *chingar* or a phrase in the *chingar* family is one of them. This word is primarily Mexican, but it is widely recognized among Spanish speakers from many countries. It means "to fuck (over)" or "to screw (over)," but it depends entirely on the context in which it is used.

Chinga tu madre is the proverbial "Fuck you!" as we say in English. Someone who screws people over, double-crosses them, or purposely causes them harm is a *chingón(a)*, but keep in mind that a *chingón(a)* can also be a "bad-ass" or a "totally cool person." Go figure. *¡Chingada madre!* is more of a general, all-purpose curse word that is not necessarily directed at anybody. *¡Chingada madre!* is something someone screams after shutting the door on his or her own finger, for example. It's the equivalent of how we might yell, "Fuck!" "Fuckin' shit!" or "Fuckin' A!" in English. *A puros chingazos* is a phrase that explains the difficulty or high cost at which something was obtained or accomplished. In English it translates to something like "the hard way" or "at a hefty price." Here's an example. Suppose you are the owner of a successful, world-renowned restaurant and someone asks you how you made it to the top. You could reply, *"¡A puros chingazos!"* as you recount how you first started in the business—washing dishes, scrubbing bathroom floors, and bussing tables. *Un chingo de* means that there is "a shitload" of something. *Hay un chingo de zapatos en oferta en la tienda* = There is a shitload of shoes on sale at the mall. If all the shoes on sale were way out of style and in bad condition, then you can refer to them as *puras chingaderas* (worthless shit). *La misma chingadera* means "the same shit." Someone asks you, "What's new?" *"La misma chingadera,"* you could respond, for example. *Hasta la quinta chingada* (or *hasta la chingada*) is dutifully employed when trying to explain that something (your house, for example) is "way the hell out there." *Meter unos chingadazos* means "to kick someone's ass." No need to explain that you probably shouldn't direct this threat at someone unless you're joking, and even then you should be cautious (see "Kick someone's ass" in chapter 5).

Cabrón(a)

Cabrón(a) is a word that sounds vulgar initially but becomes increasingly diluted the more often you hear it. *Cabrón(a)* refers to a rascal, troublemaker, or someone sneaky or shameless. A husband who stares at other women in front of his wife is a *cabrón*. The sweet, well-mannered little girl who curses at her parents in private is a *cabrona*. When spoken among friends and family, it's usually not meant to be offensive, but rather is used in a joking manner. Call your friend *cabrón* after he pulls a prank on you. When telling a story about how your friend snuck into the theater without paying, you may say, *"Este cabrón entró a escondidas al cine sin pagar"* ("This sneaky devil snuck into the theater without paying"). One may even hear *cabrón* said adoringly to a baby boy. It's not because the baby is actually a sneaky and deceitful *cabrón*, but rather because he's cute. In this sense it means "rascal."

Encabronarse (like *enojar*) is another verb for "to get angry" but more slangy. It is actually closer to "to get pissed off." You may not see this word in your textbooks, but you'll hear it all the time in conversation just as one studying

English may see "to get angry" but not "to get pissed off " in one's textbook. *Juan se encabronó cuando se enteró que su hermana salió con su mejor amigo* = Juan got pissed off when he found out that his sister went out with his best friend. *Está cabrón* is a very useful expression meaning "It's a bitch." For example, you might say, "*Está cabrón*" after explaining how far you had to walk to the nearest pay phone after your car broke down, or how many hours it took you to prepare dinner for all the guests, or even about how hard it was to loosen the lid off the pickle jar. *Está cabrón perder el trabajo en estos días* = It a bitch to lose your job in these times (days).

Pendejo(a)

A *pendejo(a)* is an idiot, or someone who does stupid or idiotic things called *pendejadas*. Someone who mistakenly puts his pants on backwards can be called a *pendejo*. A real, genuine *pendejo* would be someone who gets caught robbing the liquor store next to the police station, or someone who spends all his or her money on shorts and tanktops for a winter vacation in Antarctica. Let's say you're playing a high-stakes card game with your friends and you have the game already won. All you have to do is put down your king of spades and you win the one-hundred-dollar pot. Instead, you mistakenly put down your ace of spades (not realizing you had the game practically won) and it's just the card the guy on your right needs. He picks up the ace of spades you gave him, along with the one-hundred-dollar pot. "*¡Por pendejo!*" ("For stupidity!"), you scream as you reveal your cards to everyone, showing how *you* should have actually been the winner.

Navegar con bandera de pendejo is more of a colloquial expression describing someone who knows but pretends he or she doesn't. When Mom asks for a volunteer to get more beef from Sergio's Market, you might give her that "Where is Sergio's Market?" facial expression so that you don't get picked to go. "*Navegas con bandera de pendejo*," (literally, "You sail bearing the flag of an idiot") your mom tells you, which means "You're just playing dumb" (but you're really not). To be safe, the better and more common way of expressing this same idea is to use *hacerse pendejo(a)* (see "Play dumb" in chapter 5 for more details) or *hacerse tonto(a)*. So, instead of telling you, "*Navegas con bandera de pendejo*," it is more likely that in the previous example, your mother would say, "*No te hagas pendejo(a)*" or "*No te hagas tonto(a).*"

7

Party Training

Lingo for Living *La Vida Loca*

The topic of drinking and partying deserves a book of its own. In some circles, volumes of personal journals can be filled with tales of unforgettable late nights of loud music, impaired vision, poor judgment calls, and way too many drinks. In other circles, entire jounals are burned so that any record of wrongdoing, guilt, and embarrassment are officially pinned to the hopes of people's short-term memories—hopefully soon to be forgotten. In order to fully appreciate these unforgettable (or forgettable) moments, however, one must understand the lingo. So let's get this party started. Bottoms up!

In the door

"Let's party!" (*¡Vamos de parranda!* or *¡Hay que pachanguear!*) is what you and your friends decide. Everyone agrees to go clubbing (*ir de antro, ir a la discoteca*, or *ir al club*) and to meet at 10:00 P.M. You're the first to arrive at the club. The party is just getting started as you pay the two-hundred-peso cover charge (*la entrada*) for all you can drink at the open bar (*barra libre*) and make your way through the door. The rhythm (*ritmo*) of the music (*música*) energizes you as you start to dance (*bailar*) and scope out (*zorrear*) any potential dating possibilities while waiting for your friends to arrive. It looks like there's a good crowd that night. Hot chicks (*mamacitas*) and hot guys (*papacitos*) are everywhere, which means the competition will be stiff. You already have a few admirers (*pretendientes*) checking you out from across the room. It's time to loosen up a little and get some courage. In other words, it's time to drink (*tomar, pistiar*) and maybe even get a little drunk (*emborracharse* or *embriagarse*), so you contemplate all the options before deciding which drink (*bebida*) will turn you into the slickest, most romantic womanizer (*mujeriego*) in the room.

Loosening up

Tequila, beer (*cerveza*), a screwdriver (*desarmador*) … they all sound good, but you flag down the waiter *(el mesero)* and ask for a bucket of six ice-cold beers (*un balde de seis cervezas bien heladas*). Your friends finally arrive, fashionably late, of course. Everyone grabs a beer and says, "Cheers!" (*"¡Salud!"*). After downing several beers, your friend asks you if you're drunk. "Slightly" (*"Leve"*), you reply, but the night is young and things are just starting to heat up (*las cosas se están poniendo calientes*).

In full swing

Hours later, the party has turned into a drunken bash (*borrachera*). All the revelers raise their shot glasses. "One shot!" (*"¡Tómatelo de un jalón!"* or *"¡Un Hidalgo!"*), everyone shouts. "One shot. Screw whoever leaves anything in his shot glass!" (*"Un Hidalgo. Chingue a su madre el que deje algo"*), you add. Your friend asks you again, "How do you feel?" "Pretty drunk" (*"Bien borracho"*), you say. "I'm butt-stinking drunk" (*"Ando pedo"*), you confess more truthfully. At this point every woman looks like a goddess (*diosa*) and every man like a god (*dios*). So, with everyone looking so good and with your confidence flying high (most likely from the alcohol), you try to hook up (*ligar* or *tirar la onda*) with some prospects. After getting several telephone numbers you realize that you're a natural (*eres un nato*), that is, until you get that slap across the face (*cachetada* or *bofetada*) from that gal unwilling to relent to your advances.

The day after

You wake up the next morning with a terrible hangover (*cruda*). All you can think about is how you plan to recover (*reponerse*) over a nice steaming bowl of beef tripe soup *(menudo)*—the hangover remedy of choice in Mexico. You roll over in bed and hit something. It's your neighbor Sofía, sound asleep and snoring up a storm. You don't remember a thing, but you really prefer to leave it that way. All you can think of is how you can face your neighbor every day without feeling embarrassed. Now you have two hangovers—one hangover from the alcohol and the other a moral hangover (*cruda moral*). Note: "Hangover" is a word that is usually associated with a variety of slang terms and, therefore, tends to vary from country to country. For example, in Spain, *resaca* may be the word of choice, but in some Caribbean countries (Venezuela, for example), *ratón* (mouse) is very common. I chose *cruda* as the word for "hangover" in this section, but it is specific to Mexico and some other Latin American countries.

8

The Classified Ads
Reclassified

"Single brunette female, seeking tall, dark, handsome man." This is how you see things written in the "personals" section of the classified ads—brief, general, and mostly flattering. To the men or women reading this ad, the rest is up to their imaginations, which often create dreamy visions of statuesque supermodels just dying to pucker up and plant wet kisses all over them. In reality, we know that people don't always come so neatly packaged, nor are people so easily summarized in a few words. If we were to be completely honest in describing ourselves or others, we probably wouldn't be so select with our choice of words, though we don't usually dare to be so honest. Let's take a little break from our self-deception by creating our own classified ads. We'll call them the Classified Ads Reclassified. You'll notice that most of the words included here may not seem too flattering, but note that they are not necessarily insults either. The idea behind this chapter is not to point out the unflattering aspects of people but rather to portray these individuals as real. After all, we all have our imperfections.

Though I could not possibly have covered every human characteristic, physical feature, or personality trait, I can assure you that by learning this chapter well, your participation and understanding of conversational Spanish will jump by leaps and bounds.

Let's Get Physical

Beginning Spanish is where most of us learn the basic parts of the body and physical features called *rasgos*. As your vocabulary expands and you find yourself having more in-depth conversations with Spanish speakers, describing a mere silhouette will no longer serve your needs. Instead, you will need to become familiar with more elaborate descriptions to keep pace with your expanding dialogue. Though many of the physical descriptions listed here are a break from the traditional and customary descriptors, they are not meant to serve as a guide on how to be superficial, nor are they meant as ammunition to criticize people's appearances. Instead, they are designed to give you the tools to describe people in color rather than in black and white.

Size Matters

In this section, please make note that the Spanish words ending in "n" will have an accent over the "ó" only in the male form. If you are referring to a female, then the accent is omitted. For example, the male *nalgón, orejón,* and *cabezón* all have accents over the "ó" but the female *nalgona, orejona,* and *cabezona* do not.

Big-assed	*Nalgón(a)*
Big-bearded	*Barbón*
Big-breasted	*Chichona*
Big-eared	*Orejón(a)*
Big-footed	*Patón(a)*
Big-headed (physically)	*Cabezón(a)*
Big-lipped	*Trompudo(a)*
Big-moustached	*Bigotón*
Big-mouthed	*Bocón(a)*
Big-nosed	*Narizón(a)*
Bug-eyed	*Ojón(a)*
Bushy eyebrows	*Cejudo(a)*
Chubby-cheeked	*Cachetón(a)*
Double chin (n.)	*Papada*
Love handles (n.)	*Lonjas, Llantas, Pellas*
Potbellied	*Panzón(a)*
Thick-legged	*Piernudo(a)*
Toothy	*Dientón(a)*
Wide-hipped	*Caderón(a)*

Hairdo's and Don'ts

Afro	*Grifo*
Bald	*Pelón(a)*
Blonde	*Güero(a), Rubio(a)*
Braids	*Trenzitas*
Brunette	*Moreno(a)*
Curly hair	*Cabello chino, cabello rizado*
Gray hair(s)	*Canas*
Hairy	*Peludo(a)*
Matted, tangled hair	*Cabello enredado*
Mophead (messy hair)	*Greñudo(a)*
Redhead	*Pelirojo(a)*
Shaved head	*Cabeza rapada*
Sideburns	*Patillas*
Straight hair	*Cabello lacio*
Wavy hair	*Cabello ondulado*

Bodies of All Shapes and Sizes

Buff	*Cuadrado(a)*
Chubby	*Llenito(a)*
Fat	*Gordo(a)*
Midget	*Enano(a)*
Muscular	*Musculoso(a)*
Short	*Bajo(a), Chaparro(a)*
Skin and bones	*Calavérico(a)*
Skinny	*Flaco(a), Delgado(a)*
Slouched	*Jorobado(a)*
Tall	*Alto(a)*

Dermatology 101

Beauty mark, mole	*Lunar*
Bruise	*Morete, moretón*
Freckles	*Pecas*
Hemorrhoids	*Hemorroides, almorranas*
Pimple	*Grano*
Sun spots	*Manchas del sol*
Sunburned	*Quemado(a) del sol*
Tan	*Bronceado(a)*
Tattoo	*Tatuaje*
Wart	*Verruga*
Wrinkles	*Arrugas*

Sticks and Stones

Talking about people—who they are, who they aren't, what you think of them, and what people say about them—will always be a juicy topic. Name-calling, or labeling, is how we do it. So unless you can understand the terminology used to categorize and generalize about people, you'll never be fully involved in some of the juiciest conversations life has to offer. Here's your chance.

In this section, please make note that many of the Spanish adjectives and nouns ending in "n" will have an accent over the "ó" only in the male form. If you are referring to a female, then the accent is omitted. For example, the male *bocón, chingón,* and *sangrón* all have accents over the "ó" but the female *bocona, chingona,* and *sangrona* do not.

Important reminder:

Before beginning this section, be sure to review Rule #4 of "Housekeeping Rules" in Chapter 2.

Abusive	*Abusivo(a), Colgado(a)* (adj. and n.)
	Abusivo(a) is the general and universal word for "abusive." It can refer to physical abuse and mental abuse, but it also refers to people who abuse privileges afforded to them. *Un(a) colgado(a)*, which is a more Mexican term, is a cross between a leech and an opportunist, but neither is strong enough to describe this individual because someone who is *colgado(a)* is the extreme version of both rolled into one. This term describes someone who is abusive by excessively taking advantage of other people. Ask *un colgado* if he wants to try some of your steak and he'll help himself to half of your meat. Let him borrow your shirt and you'll never see it again.

Airhead   ***Cabeza hueca*** (n.)

Cabeza hueca literally means "hollow head" but it is the Spanish-language version of our "airhead." A *cabeza hueca*, for example, might believe you if you said that buffalo wings are actually made of buffalo, or that mothballs come from flying-insect genitalia.

Annoying   ***Enfadoso(a), Chocante*** (adj. and n.)
                               Engorroso(a) (adj.)

Pesty people who fall into this category can get underneath your skin. They badger, nag, and frustrate you, and no repellant will protect you from their irritation. *Enfadoso(a)* is by far the most commonly used term, while you may hear the words *engorroso(a)* and *chocante* only occasionally.

Arrogant   ***Arrogante, Presumido(a), Engreído(a),
                               Soberbio(a), Sangrón(a)***

(All are used as adjectives and nouns except *soberbio(a)*, which is only an adjective.)

You may have noticed that there are several words to describe someone who is arrogant. The adjectives listed above describe someone who is stuck-up, pompous, arrogant, snobby, and/or self-absorbed. *Arrogante, presumido(a)*, and the noun *sangrón(a)* are used all the time in conversation.

Baby   ***Chiquiado(a)*** (adj. and n.)

Bebé is "baby" as you know. Someone who is not a baby but acts or talks like a baby is being *chiquiado(a)*. Your significant other might talk *chiquiado(a)* when he or she wants something from you.

Bad energy   ***Sangre pesada*** (adj. and n.)

Someone who has *sangre pesada* (heavy blood) has an abrasive tone or gives off a negative vibe. This person seems to always rub people the wrong way, whether it is intentional or not. Call it unfair but sometimes a person can be called *sangre pesada* just because of the way he or she looks.

Bad-ass   ***Chingón(a)*** (adj. and n.)

The smooth-talking, moon-walking individual who is too cool, and knows it. This term can also describe someone who excels in a subject or activity. It is important to recognize the context in which this term is used because a *chingón(a)* can also describe someone who screws people over.

Badgering   ***Calilla*** (adj. and n.)

Have you ever met someone who just won't stop badgering or pestering you with question after question or demand after demand? That person can be described as *calilla*. When getting ready to go to a party, the *calilla* will be the one telling you, "Let's go, let's go already!" practically pushing you out the door. Note: this word will always take the feminine ending "a" but that doesn't mean this word applies only to females, as we all know men can also be labeled as such.

Bigmouth   ***Bocón(a)*** (adj. and n.)

A *bocón(a)* is a bigmouth. This type talks too much, talks too loudly, or has a tendency to blurt out inappropriate comments at the inappropriate time. This can also describe someone who has a rated-R mouth and whose verbal vulgarisms and profanity are better off bleeped out of the conversation.

Bitter   ***Amargado(a)*** (adj. and n.)

Bitter-tasting food is described as *amargo(a)*, but an embittered person is described as *amargado(a)*.

Bossy   ***Mandón(a)*** (adj. and n.)

The *mandón(a)* is demanding and pushy and may also be described as a control freak. He or she gives the orders and cracks the whip. This adjective is derived from the verb *mandar*, which means "to command" or "to order."

Brave   ***Valiente*** (adj. and n.)

The woman who jumps in front of her trembling husband when the intimidating bully comes rushing in is *valiente*. The husband can be called a *cobarde*, *culón(a)*, or *caguetas* (the two latter terms are crude).

Bully   ***Bravucón(a)*** (adj. and n.)

The *bravucón(a)* is just looking for a scuffle and is ready to fight anyone, anytime.

Caring	***Cariñoso(a)*** (adj.) A person who is *cariñoso(a)* is warm, caring, and affectionate. This type may give you a lot of hugs and kisses, along with soothing words of love or encouragement. Not on the endangered species list yet, but a rare find these days.
Chatterbox	***Platicador(a), Cotorra*** (adj. and n.) Has a high-octane motormouth running on autopilot. You might want to have an escape route or evacuation plan when confronted with this type.
Cheater	***Chapucero(a)*** (adj. and n.) Cutting corners and playing dirty is what the *chapucero(a)* does best in order to gain the upper hand in games, competitions, and exams. This term does not apply to cheating on one's lover.
Chickenshit, Coward	***Caguetas, Cagón(a), Culón(a), Cobarde, Tameme*** (adj. and n.) If someone calls you by one of the terms listed above, the person is saying that you're a coward. *Cobarde* and *tameme* are less offensive terms (*tameme* is less universal than *cobarde*), and *caguetas, cagón(a),* and *culón(a)* are definitely cruder, referring to a "shitter" of sorts, much like the English "chickenshit." *Miedoso(a)* (scared) is the adjective to describe this person.

Clueless   ***Buenas tardes*** (adj.)

As we learned in chapter 3, *buenas tardes* means "good afternoon." *Buenas tardes,* however, is also a slang term used to describe clueless individuals who are unconcerned, distracted, and oblivious to the world around them. These persons epitomize the saying "Ignorance is bliss," because they are happier not knowing what's going on. For example, you can say, *"Ese muchacho es muy buenas tardes"* ("This guy is so clueless") about the guy driving at a snail's pace on the freeway while talking to a friend on his cell phone, looking at all the stores on the side of the road, and slowing down and changing lanes at his leisure without a reason or regard for other drivers.

Clumsy   ***Torpe*** (adj. and n.)

A person who is *torpe* is clumsy and clutzy and prone to tripping, bumping into people and things, and dropping things. Make sure to childproof your house before this type comes over.

Competitive   ***Gandalla*** (adj. and n.)

Disclaimer: *Gandalla* is not the general, all-purpose word for "competitive." It actually describes a person who has a somewhat greedy desire to be the first, and will even take advantage of people or situations in order to get there. *Una persona gandalla,* which can refer to a male or a female, always has to be the first to know what's going on, the first in line, the first to wear the newest fashion trends, and so on.

Conceited

Presumido(a) (adj. and n.)

Characterized by habitual self-glorification, the *presumido(a)* has a lot of pride and will unabashedly let you know it by publicly tooting his or her own horn.

Confrontational

Peleonero(a) (adj. and n.)

A person described as *peleonero(a)* is inclined to fighting or instigating fights and arguments. He or she is often just conflict driven and needs a daily dose of quarreling in order to make it through the day.

Grillero(a) (adj. and n.)

Someone described as *grillero(a)* is confrontational in a work environment. Concerned more about rights, fairness, and equality than productivity and efficiency, this type may say, "I won't do anything else unless they pay me extra," or "I'm not obligated to work even a second over my normal working hours." A union rep can be *grillero(a),* for example. Though sometimes it's necessary for an employee to set limits with his or her boss, most employers view *grilleros(as)* as counterproductive nuisances in the workplace.

Conniving

Sisañoso(a) (adj. and n.)

Keep in mind that someone who is considered *sisañoso(a)* is secretly conniving by planting the seed that causes the controversy or fight, and then "innocently" leaves the scene of the crime to watch events unfold from the sidelines.

Cool   ***Buena onda, Padre, Chido(a), Chilo(a)***
                         (adj.)

                         Cool people are *buena onda*, but cool or awesome
                         things or events are described as *padre, chido(a),
                         or chilo(a)*. *Mi hermano es muy buena onda* = My
                         brother is really cool. When referring to that cool
                         new movie that just came out, for example, then
                         use *padre, chido(a),* or *chilo(a)*. *¡Esa nueva
                         película está padre!* = That new movie is totally
                         cool!

Copy cat   ***Copión(a)*** (adj. and n.)

                         The younger tag-along sibling who always
                         repeats or imitates the actions, words,
                         appearances, or mannerisms of the older brother
                         is an example of a *copión(a)*.

Corny   ***Simple*** (adj.)

                         Simple in Spanish is pronounced as *SEEm-pleh*
                         (not *SIM-pul*). It describes someone who is silly
                         or funny but in a more subtle, cheesy, or corny
                         way.

Disloyal   ***Chaquetero(a)*** (adj. and n.)

                         Chaquetero(a) doesn't mean "disloyal" in the
                         pure sense of the word. Colloquially, it describes
                         someone who has changed sides and it refers
                         mainly to people who switch loyalties based on
                         what is popular. A person who jumps on the
                         bandwagon of the winning team can be described
                         as *chaquetero(a)*.

Dull

Insípido(a) (adj.)

A person with no personality, a dull and uninspiring performance, a boring movie, and even tasteless food can all be described as *insípido(a)*.

Fake

Falso(a), Fingido(a) (adj. and n.)

A person who is *falso(a)* or *fingido(a)* wears many faces but rarely his or her own (at least in public). Usually the person projects an impression to other people other than that of who he or she really is. (Also see "Two-faced" later in this chapter.)

Faker

Farsante (adj. and n.)

A *farsante* is a "faker" or a "fraud," like someone faking an injury for attention (seen any professional soccer matches lately?). It can also be a scam artist who takes payment for goods and has no intention of actually delivering them.

Disimulado(a) (adj. and n.)

Someone described as *disimulado(a)* is a faker of a different sort. This type of faker selectively hears and notices things depending on what is personally convenient. For example, he or she might pretend not to notice everyone at the party helping out just to get out of having to pitch in. This type may also pretend not to hear a coworker asking for assistance so that someone else can sacrifice his or her time by helping out instead.

Favorite   ***Consentido(a)*** (adj. and n.)

The favorite, the "chosen one," or that special person that one holds most dear to one's heart. "Daddy's girl" and "mama's boy" are good examples of this.

Flake   ***Rajón(a)*** (adj. and n.), ***Pájaro nalgón*** (n.)

In English a "flake" is simply someone who backs out of a promise or obligation. In Spanish (particularly in Mexico) flakes fall into two categories: *formal* and *informal*. The elusive *rajón(a)* would be the formal flake who makes mutually agreed upon plans and then backs out of them. The *pájaro nalgón* is the informal flake because he or she doesn't make formal plans or promises. Instead, the *pájaro nalgón* wants to be the crowd pleaser by saying, "Yes" to almost everything but in the end pleases no one because he or she hardly ever honors a commitment.

Flirt   ***Coqueto(a), Pajuelo(a)*** (adj. and n.)

Showing off the butt and batting the eyelashes are all in the arsenal of a person described as *coqueto(a)* or *pajuelo(a)*. Between the two, *coqueto(a)* is the more commonly used term in conversation. Both *coqueto(a)* and *pajuelo(a)* are used as adjectives and nouns. Therefore, *eres muy coqueto(a)* (You're very flirtatious) and *eres un coqueto(a)* (You're a flirt) are grammatically correct. The same applies to the word *pajuelo(a)*.

Funny   ***Chistoso(a), Curado(a)*** (adj.)

Both of these terms are good words to describe someone or something humorous. Funny people, movies, and jokes can all be referred to with the adjectives *chistosos(as)* or *curados(as)*.

Good-looking   ***Bonito(a), Guapo(a), Cuero*** (adj.)

Since beauty is in the eye of the beholder, these terms are entirely subjective, but they generally refer to someone who is handsome, pretty, cute, or beautiful. *Bonito(a)* and *guapo(a)* are universal definitions, whereas *cuero(a)* is heard more in Mexico. You're probably better off sticking with the more universal terms since *cuero(a)* can mean good-looking as an adjective, or an old bag, old hag, whore, lover, wallet, or skin as a noun. These meanings vary depending on which Spanish-speaking country you're from. "Skin" is the only universal translation.

Goody-two-shoes   ***Santurrón(a)*** (adj. and n.)

Santurrón(a) is an interesting word because it has two equally valid definitions: one definition that can be interpreted as positive and one as negative. It means saintly, churchgoing, God-fearing, law-abiding, straight as an arrow, and prim and proper. It also means holier-than-thou or hypocritical. So, if someones calls you *santurrón(a)*, you might want to ask for clarification on which definition of the word is intended.

Greedy   ***Basto(a), Goloso(a), Lángaro(a)***
                         (adj. and n.)

Greedy and selfish, with a tendency to hoard or take more than one needs. This term is often used to describe someone who is greedy about food. *Eres basto(a)* = You're greedy.

Grouch

Cascarrabias (n.)

This is a good term to call a cranky, crabby, quick-tempered person known for frequent griping and infrequent smiling. *Eres un(a) cascarrabias* = You're a grouch.

Guinea pig

Conejillo de Indias (n.)

The *conejillo de Indias* is the one chosen to be the first to try something in order to ensure that it is safe for everyone else. This person would be the first to test the new experimental medicine or even the concoction your mother just whipped up for dinner.

Gullible

Inocente (adj. and n.)

In English the word "gullible" sounds a little condescending because it has come to mean that someone is a bit of a sucker. In Spanish the word for gullible is *inocente,* which is less harsh because it leans more towards being naive than towards being a sucker. Note: *El Día de los Inocentes* is the equivalent of our April Fools' Day.

Haggard

Ojeroso(a) (adj.)

This one doesn't really refer to an overall haggard appearance but more specifically to the dark circles around the eyes that result from lack of sleep or age. *Ojeroso(a)* comes from the word *ojos* (eyes).

Hard-core **De hueso colorado** (adj.)

This entry describes someone having an un-inhibited and unrestrained passion for something. Hard-core fans of any sport (*aficionados de hueso colorado* = hard-core fans) might have season tickets, posters adorning their rooms, and all the apparel of their favorite teams. Someone asks if you're a fan of baseball. You can reply, "*Sí, soy de hueso colorado*" ("Yes, I'm hard-core").

Horny **Cachondo(a), Caliente, Excitado(a)** (adj.)

Someone who is *cachondo(a)* (horny) has his or her hormones revved up full throttle and is typically looking for (or thinking about) sexual activity of some sort. Other common terms for "horny" are *caliente* and *excitado(a)*.

Hyperactive **Acelerado(a)** (adj.)

This word describes someone who is restless, jumpy, overactive and impatient. This type often does things at an accelerated, even desperate pace.

Idiot **Idiota, Pendejo(a), Baboso(a), Tonto(a)** (adj. and n.)

Every village has an idiot, including villages in Latin America. These terms are closely related and can all be used to say, "idiot." There are, however, a few noteworthy distinctions. The more universal term, *idiota,* has a harsher tone. *Pendejo(a)* can have a harsh tone but is also used loosely and jokingly among friends. A person who is an idiot can also be called a *baboso(a)* or a *tonto(a),* but these two terms lean closer to "fool," which tends to sound less derogatory.

Jealous

Envidioso(a), Celoso(a) (adj.)

Both *envidioso(a)* and *celoso(a)* mean "jealous," but they are not used interchangeably. *Celoso(a)* typically refers to relationships such as with a jealous husband or wife, for example. *Soy muy celosa y no me gusta que mi esposo salga solo en la noche* = I'm very jealous and I don't like my husband going out alone at night. *Envidioso(a)* describes jealousy of your friend's new car or high-paying job, for example. It is often expressed in the noun form *(envidia)* with the verb *dar* (to give). *Me da envidia tu carro nuevo* = I'm jealous of your new car. If your jealousy is well intentioned and not malicious in nature, then add *de la buena* at the end. This means "in a good way." *Me da envidia tu carro nuevo, pero envidia de la buena* = I'm jealous of your new car, but in a good way.

Kiss-ass

Barbero(a), Lambiscón(a) (adj. and n.)

Of the two terms listed, *barbero(a)* should be your first choice since it is more familiar to most Spanish speakers. It means "kiss-ass," "brownnoser," and in a classroom setting, "teacher's pet." The *barbero(a)* specializes in paying compliments and buttering people up in order to win their favor.

Know-it-all

Sabelotodo (adj. and n.)

Some people actually do seem to know it all, but usually a *sabelotodo* only *thinks* he or she knows it all.

Lazy ass

Huevón(a) (adj. and n.)

A *huevón(a)* is a lazy person or "lazy ass" as is frequently heard in English. The adjective to describe a *huevón(a)* is *flojo(a)* or *flojera*.

Leech

Vividor(a), Gorrón(a) (adj. and n.)

A *vividor(a)* or *gorrón(a)* is the Spanish-language version of the "freeloader" or "moocher." This person is a parasite who lives and feeds off of other people, like the guy who eats all your food without pitching in a dime, or the person who invites himself over to your house and then decides to stay for a few more days.

Pediche (adj. and n.)

The *pediche* is a different species of leech. Though not the one who takes and takes without giving back, the *pediche* constantly asks for things (but doesn't necessarily get them). "Can I see that?" "Can I try one of those?" "Can you take me there?" Hint: The word *pediche* is derived from the verb *pedir* (to ask for).

Liar

Mentiroso(a), Embustero(a) (adj. and n.)

Both *mentiroso(a)* and *embustero(a)* mean liar or trickster but *mentiroso(a)* is the more universal term between the two.

Loser

Mequetrefe (n.)

You won't hear this word all that often simply because it is considered to be an offensive term. *Mequetrefe* means "loser" and nobody likes to be called a loser. This term is closely related to *títere* and *pelele*, which both mean "pushover." In fact, native speakers often use all three of these terms interchangeably.

Mama's boy syndrome *Mamitis* (n.)

Someone who has *mamitis* is a mama's boy. *Mamitis* is a condition whose main symptom is an overreliance on one's mother. Technically, girls can also have *mamitis,* but it almost always refers to males.

Moody   *Voluble* (adj.)

This fickle individual is unpredictably up and down with emotions. Like a sunny day that suddenly turns stormy, someone who is *voluble* is happy one minute and agitated the next.

Naive   *Ingenuo(a)* (adj. and n.)

The often innocent and unsuspecting person described as *ingenuo(a)* is sometimes oblivious to what many would consider the practical or common-knowledge realities of life. Not to be confused with an idiot or the like, *ingenuo(a)* usually refers to a person who is young, sheltered, or just inexperienced.

Nobody   *Don nadie* (n.)

The "nobody" in a room full of "somebodies." The *don nadie* considers himself or herself to be a person of high standing or power. What makes this person a *don nadie,* however, is the fact that nobody else agrees with his or her elevated sense of importance.

Nosy

Entrometido(a), Mitotero(a), Metiche
(adj. and n.)

The *metiche* is a nosy person described by the adjectives *entrometido(a)* and *mitotero(a)*. Such super-snoopers make everyone else's business their business by sticking their noses where they don't belong and following the scent of anything resembling gossip (*chisme*).

Opportunist

Oportunista, Aprovechador(a) (n.)

Someone who takes advantage (sometimes excessively) of opportunities is an *oportunista* or *aprovechador(a)*. If there's a hole, the *oportunista* will find a way through it, but he or she doesn't necessarily do this at the expense of others. See the term "abusive" at the beginning of this chapter to learn more about the extreme opportunist.

Pack rat

Tilichero(a) (adj. and n.)

The extreme collector of often less-than-collectable things, the *tilichero(a)* doesn't throw things away but instead will store them or pile them up even if they are never to be used or seen again.

Party crasher

Colado(a), Gorrón(a) (adj. and n.)

Un(a) colado(a) is an uninvited guest, a party crasher, and even someone who cuts in line at the movie theater. A *gorrón(a)* is the same as a *colado(a)*, but as you may recall, *gorrón(a)* also refers to a "leech" (see "leech" earlier in this chapter).

Party pooper

Aguafiestas (n.)

The "wet blanket" or "killjoy" of the group, the *aguafiestas* might dampen the mood by leaving the party early or by refusing to participate in the festivities.

Picky

Exigente (adj. and n.)

Someone who is picky or hard to please would be described as *exigente* in Spanish. This type of person orders a burger with cheese on one half, ketchup on the side, the top bun grilled, and the bottom bun toasted. *Poner los moños* (to put on ribbons or bows) also means "to be picky" but with a splash of perfectionism. For instance, your interior designer has done a fabulous job on your house, but although perfect by most standards, there are always last-minute changes you want to introduce. Apologetically, you may say, *"No es que me quiera poner los moños, pero no estoy satisfecho totalmente"* ("It's not that I am trying to be too picky, but I'm not really totally satisfied").

Pig

Cochino(a) (adj. and n.)

If someone calls you a *cochino* (pig), it doesn't mean that you eat a lot but it could mean that you spill your food all over your clothes when you do eat. A *cochino(a)* is a dirty, messy slob. Possible symptoms might include a filthy room, infrequent bathing, and an unkempt appearance.

Tragón(a), Comelón(a) (adj. and n.)

If you want to call someone a pig because he or she eats too much, then use the term *tragón(a)* from the verb *tragar* (to swallow), or *comelón* from the verb *comer* (to eat). It means a "human garbage can."

Playful

Jugetón(a) (adj.)

A puppy chasing his caretaker around the backyard or a little boy chasing his classmates around the playground are examples of someone who is playful, or *jugetón(a)*, as they say in Spanish.

Pushover

Títere, Pelele (n.)

A *títere* is a marionette or puppet and a *pelele* is a ragdoll, so you can imagine that someone described as a *títere* or *pelele* is a spineless pushover and moves to the will of whoever is pulling the strings.

Rough

Tosco(a) (adj.)

The big, burly guy in the class who seems to be too big for his age and who doesn't know his own strength. Someone who is *tosco* may affectionately pat his friend on the back and unintentionally knock him down. *Tosco(a)* can also mean "rough around the edges" or having crude mannerisms.

Rude

Grosero(a) (adj. and n.)

Offensive, improper, and unrefined in one's words or actions, like burping at the dinner table in the presence of guests or insulting people without reason.

Scapegoat

Chivo expiatorio (n.)

The "fall guy" chosen to take the blame on behalf of the group.

Scummy

Cuachalote(a) (adj. and n.)
Chirangudo(a), Desmelechado(a) (adj.)

Filthy, dirty, unkempt. These terms are more specific to someone's physical appearance unlike the more broadly defined *cochino(a)*—though you can also feel free to use *cochino* to describe someone who is physically filthy, dirty, and unkempt. For example, someone who dresses like a bum in sweatpants and a T-shirt with holes or someone who goes out with his or her hair sticking up in all directions could be called *cuachalote(a)* or *chirangudo(a)* in Mexico, and is commonly referred to as *desmelechado(a)* in some parts of Central America.

Self-serving

Interesado(a) (adj. and n.)

These individuals are always looking out for number one—themselves. Often referred to as "gold diggers," they do not concern themselves with obtaining the superfluous luxuries of life. That's because they might be looking for a sugar daddy or sugar mama to do it for them.

Shitty

Chafa (adj.)

Chafa means junky, shitty, or of poor quality like that cheap watch that stops working every five minutes. *La comida está chafa* means that the food is shitty or practically inedible. *Esos aretes se ven chafas* = Those earrings look cheap. Note: the term *chafa* always takes the feminine *a* ending.

Show-off

Fachoso(a) (adj. and n.)

Describes someone who puts on a show for other people to impress them or draw attention. An example of this would be that wanna-be who overdoes it by wearing trendy sunglasses, way too much gold on his hairy chest, and all the latest and most expensive brand names in fashion.

Slut

Trepadora, Cascos livianos, Coscolina (n.)

Literally, a *trepadora* is a climbing plant, so it makes sense that figuratively it is a woman who climbs in bed with men in order to climb up the ranks in her career. The terms *coscolina* and *cascos livianos* (light helmets) refer to someone who is "loose," and is said about someone who "gives it up" without much of a chase.

Spoiled

Mimado(a), Fresa (adj. and n.)

Spoiled food is *podrido* but a spoiled child, for example, is *mimado(a)*. A spoiled female who is used to everyone doing things for her can be called *fresa* (strawberry). Though the word *fresa* is a noun, it is used as an adjective when describing spoiled people. *Ella es muy fresa* = She is very spoiled.

Spoiler

Regasón(a) (adj. and n.)

Nearly synonymous with the party pooper (*aguafiestas*). A *regasón(a)* would ruin the surprise, spill the beans, spoil the mood, or take the fun out of something.

Stingy

Agarrado(a), Codo(a), Tacaño(a)
(adj. and n.)

These adjectives describe someone who has enough money, food, etc., but doesn't want to share it even when obligated to do so. This type, often called a cheapskate, doesn't have to be thrifty out of necessity as perhaps a poor college student would. The millionaire who won't tip only because it's a few extra dollars out of his or her pocket would be considered *codo(a)*, *agarrado(a)*, or *tacaño(a)*. It is interesting to note that since the word *codo(a)* literally means "elbow," you may see someone simply touch his or her elbow to indicate that someone is stingy without actually having to voice this sentiment.

Storyteller

Cuentero(a) (adj. and n.)

A *cuentero(a)* is a storyteller. What kind of storyteller is totally dependent on who is telling the story. It can be someone who tells it like it is in such a way that captivates listeners while not straying from the truth, or it can also describe someone who exaggerates, distorts, or outright invents a story.

Stubborn

Terco(a) (adj. and n.)

If we made comparisons to the animal kingdom, this individual would be like the mule (*burro*) of our species.

Alegativo(a) (adj. and n.)

A man described as *terco* may be stubborn, but it doesn't necessarily mean that he is wrong or unreasonable in his stubborness. A woman described as *alegativa*, however, is also stubborn but she is unrelentingly insistent and won't stop until you see things her way—even if she's wrong.

Suffocating

Encimoso(a) (adj. and n.)

Much like a stuffy sinus congestion, someone who is *encimoso(a)* doesn't let you breathe. This type is always looking over your shoulder, breathing down your neck, or crowding upon your personal space. *Mi perro es muy encimoso porque por donde volteo, ahí está* = My dog is so suffocating because wherever I turn, there he is.

Tacky

Cursi (adj. and n.)

Cursi means "of poor taste," "tacky," or "cheesy." That tacky fluorescent pink sweater with black polka dots would be considered *cursi* among other things. So would that guy who is always trying to win over his love interest with sappy love poems.

Teasing

Carrilludo(a), Llevado(a) (adj. and n.)

An older sister who picks on or makes fun of her younger brother can be described as *carilluda* or *llevada*.

Thick-skinned

Conchudo(a) (adj. and n.)

Hardened and callous are the traditional definitions in English, but Spanish has taken it one step further to also include people who are plain lazy, too comfortable to lift a finger, and too thick-skinned to give a damn about their behavior.

Trashy

Corriente (adj. and n.), ***Naco(a)*** (n.)

A *naco(a)* refers to someone who lacks class and may come across as grossly unrefined, uneducated, disrespectful, and rough around the edges. *Corriente* is the adjective that describes this type; however, *corriente* also refers to things—not just people. Things perceived as being of lower quality or class, such as low-quality clothes and fast food, for example, can also be called *corriente*.

Troublemaker

Travieso(a), Vago(a) (adj. and n.)

A person described as a *vago(a)* is a troublemaker who bothers others or gets into mischief. This type can be anyone from a gangster (*cholo*) to a little boy getting into everything. Someone described as *travieso(a)* is a slightly watered-down and more innocent version of the *vago(a)*. It usually refers specifically to mischievous children.

Two-faced individual

Hipócrita (adj. and n.), ***Dos caras*** (n.)

These terms refer to a hypocritical, untrustworthy individual who speaks kindly in your face and disparagingly behind your back. Can also be described as a "backstabber."

Mosquita muerta (n.)

Though males also exhibit characteristics of the *mosquita muerta,* for some reason, this term only refers to females. *Mosquita muerta* means "little dead fly." In the insect world, a little dead fly is harmless. A person who falls into this category, however, is far from harmless. The *mosquita muerta* is selfish and calculating but you probably won't realize it at first. This type will do things that offend you but will feel no obligation whatsoever to give any rhyme or reason for her actions. Then, in your presence, she will put on a sweet and innocent *cara de yo no fui* ("it wasn't me" face) and thinks you are stupid enough to be fooled by it. The worst thing about this shameless, manipulating individual is that she has the nerve to actually play it off and smile at everyone she has wronged as if to convince the wronged individuals that they are only imagining or misinterpreting any offensive behavior committed against them.

Unattached

Despegado(a) (adj.)

By choice, the individual who is *despegado(a)* prefers to keep an arm's length between himself or herself and other people. It could be due to friction between both parties or simply a privacy issue. Whatever the reason, someone who is *despegado(a)* would just rather not get too close to all of the action.

Ungrateful

Malagradecido(a) (adj. and n.)

Someone described as *malagradecido(a)* is difficult to please because this person is usually unappreciative and quite selfish. It seems like nothing is good enough to make this type of person happy or grateful.

Unstoppable

Imparable (adj.)

The thunderous avalanche, the insurmountable tidal wave, the all-powerful superhero, the basketball player who nobody can guard are all *imparable*.

Walking disaster   ***Contingente*** (adj. and n.)

Every day is like Friday the thirteenth for the *contingente* because this type is perpetually prone to sickness, accidents, and bad luck.

Weakling   ***Ñengo(a)*** (n.)

A *ñengo(a)* is someone who is physically weak, scrawny, uncoordinated, and frail in stature.

Whipped individual   ***Mandilón*** (adj. and n.)

A *mandil* is an apron. A *mandilón* refers to a male who wears the apron instead of the pants. A *mandilón* usually needs permission from his wife or girlfriend before going out and is often defined by the phrase "Yes, dear."

Whore   ***Una Cualquiera*** (n.)

Una cualquiera is a whore. This entry serves as fair warning that this term is very offensive and should not be used.

Womanizer   ***Mujeriego*** (adj. and n.)

A *mujeriego* is a smooth-talking, slick ladies' man who knows exactly how to bait and reel in the women.

Terms of Endearment

Not all name-calling is offensive, thank goodness. Our loved ones and even our "liked ones" need names, too, and Spanish offers its own unique list of affectionate titles for everyone who matters to us. Below you will find some of the most frequently used terms of endearment. For most of them, you can add the suffix *-ito* or *-cito* (for males) and an *-ita* or *-cita* (for females), and it makes these titles even more endearing, as if blowing a little kiss at the end or adding a little cherry on top.

Amor	**Love**
	Truly, love is an international language of its own and this term is the foundation for all of the endearing titles to follow. We address people whom we love with *mi amor* (my love). Such people could include husbands, wives, boyfriends, girlfriends, and children (even if they're not your own). Though we love our parents and grandparents, we do not address them with *amor*.
Bebé	**Baby**
	Bebé is just what it sounds like—"baby." Parents address their own children with *bebé*, but quite often you will also hear lovey-dovey couples use this term with each other, too.
Carnal	**Bro**
	You'll hear this one on the streets among close male friends. *Carnal* translates to "carnal" or "of the flesh" but it is the equivalent of our "bro" or "brother," and males can say it to other males they consider to be flesh and blood regardless if they're actually related or not.
Chico(a)	**Guy, Girl**
	This one is often heard in a greeting like ¡*Hola chico!* or ¡*Hola chica!* It means "Hey, guy!" or "Hey, girl!" and is typically spoken among the younger crowd. It is especially used informally among friends, cousins, and peers.

Cielo   **Heaven**

This is another one of the more endearing terms in line with *amor* and *bebé*. One might hear *mi cielo* (my heaven) addressed to someone believed to be heavenly or not of this earth. Adoring mothers might say this to their children, grandparents to their grandchildren, and loving wives and husbands to each other.

Comadre   **Buddy (female)**

If Elena is the godmother of Raquel's child, for example, then she is the *comadre* (like a second mother). Elena and Raquel can address each other by this term instead of using their real names. Informally, however, women can say this to close female friends or to someone with whom they feel a special friendly bond or connection, in which case "buddy" or "sister" becomes the better translation.

Compadre   **Buddy (male)**

This is the same thing as *comadre* above, but for the male gender.

Corazón   **Sweetheart**

You may already know that *corazón* means "heart," but when you call someone *corazón* endearingly, the more accurate translation is closer to our English equivalent of "sweetheart."

Curioso(a)   **Cute**

Curioso can also mean "curious," "interesting," and "peculiar," and though someone who is *curioso(a)* may possess these qualities, it usually means "cute" or "darling" when referring to people. *Mira qué curioso se ve ese niño jugando con la pelota* = Look how cute this boy looks playing with the ball.

Divino(a)   **Divine, Wonderful**

Like *cielo(a)*, we say someone is *divino(a)* when the person is just too precious to be of this earth. This one is reserved for our precious children, that adorable puppy, and even that hot chick or steamy hunk with whom you are fascinated. *¡Está divino el muchacho que conocí en la fiesta!* = The guy that I met at the party is wonderful!

Dulce   **Sweetie**

This one is less commonly heard than many of the others, but you can't go wrong in saying this to someone you adore. Besides, who wouldn't love to be called "sweetie"?

Flaco(a)   **Skinny**

Flaco(a) means skinny but you certainly don't have to be skin and bones for someone to say it to you. Spoken affectionately, it is like saying, *"Mi amor"* (My love). So don't worry—your loved one won't ask you to step on the scale to confirm if you qualify to be called *flaco(a)*.

Gordo(a)   **Fatty, Fatso**

In the identical way that *flaco(a)* is used in the above example, the same thing applies to *gordo(a)*. Though it may sound insulting and rude to you, it is not so in Latino culture. A husband may publicly call his wife *gorda* and a wife may call her husband *gordo* without remorse or thinking twice. In fact, I heard someone say, "My wife calls me *gordo* when she wants something from me." Again, it doesn't matter if you really are *gordo(a)* or not. You can actually be as skinny as a pole and still be lovingly referred to as *gordo* by your wife. By the way, don't be surprised to hear babies referred to as *gordos(as)*. It is quite common.

Güey   **Dude, Man**

Güey is a unisex "Mexicanismo" that's as common as they come. Though it may come across as something only a man would say to another man, this is not the case. Both men *and* women can refer to other men or women as *güeyes,* but please refrain from addressing more formal company by this term. Some people seem to saturate every sentence with the word *güey.* The definition is somewhat tough to pinpoint, but it is used similarly to how the omnipresent "dude" or "man" is used in English. *Mira, güey, te digo que no vas a poder entrar a la discoteca, güey, porque está lleno hasta la puerta, güey* = Look, dude, I tell you that you won't be able to get into the discotheque, man, because it's packed to the door, dude. Not to be confused with *buey,* which means ox or steer.

Hijo(a)   **Son, Daughter**

Hijo(a) means son or daughter (depending on the ending, of course), but one can say this affectionately to any child even if he or she is not one's own. Husbands and wives can even say this affectionately to each other.

Hombre   **Man**

Hombre is casual, mild street talk for "man," as commonly heard in English. *¿Qué pasa, hombre?* = What's up, man? For example, José dares you to shoot a spitball at the teacher, so you respond with, *"¿Estás loco, hombre?"* ("Are you crazy, man?").

Mamacita   **Babe, Hot mama, Mom**
Mami
Mamá   *Mamacita, mami,* and *mamá* are all terms that lustful men might shout out to a beautiful woman walking across the street. They translate to "babe" or "hot mama," and they are definite "come-ons" in this context. A child, however, can also address his or her mother by the terms *mami* and *mamá,* but certainly not by *mamacita,* which is widely interpreted as having sexual overtones.

Mi vida   **My life**

This is the ultimate feel-good title. If someone addresses you as *"Mi vida,"* you should be flattered because you are loved. It means "My life" and you don't just say this to anyone.

Mijo(a)   **My son, My daughter**

Mijo(a) refers to a son or daughter just like *hijo(a)*, but like many of the terms in this section, it is not limited to children. It is actually a contraction of the words *mi hijo* or *mi hija* and means "my son" or "my daughter." Say this to anyone younger than you whom you consider to be like your own child.

Morro(a)   **Dude, Chick**

A very informal and slangy Mexican term for "dude" or "chick," of course depending on which gender you're addressing. *¿Qué ondas, morra?* = What's up, chick? Keep in mind that you can also replace *morro(a)* with the unisex *güey.*

Nene, Nena   **Baby**

Nene is a synonym for *bebé,* but in conversation it seems to be spoken more endearingly than *bebé. Nene* is a unisex term and can refer to either a female or male, but you will also hear *nena,* which refers only to females.

Niño(a)   **Child**

This is a common way to address any child, including childish adults who sometimes forget how old they are.

Papacito   **Babe, Hunk, Dad**
Papi
Papá   *Papacito, papi,* and *papá* are the male equivalents of the
                female *mamacita, mami,* and *mamá.* Adoring fans can
                refer to that handsome daytime soap opera hunk as
                papacito, papi, and *papá.* Children often call their father
                papi or *papá,* but never *papacito.* Like the term *mamacita,*
                the word *papacito* is also widely interpreted as having
                sexual overtones.

Precioso(a) **Precious**

                It doesn't take a rocket scientist to figure this one out.
                Precioso(a) is simply "precious," and like so many of the
                other endearing titles in this section, this one is usually
                directed towards children and lovebirds.

Querido(a) **Dear, Darling, Beloved**

                Querido(a) means "dear," "darling," or "beloved." In
                Spanish we say this to people we hold dear to our hearts.
                Personal letters to a good friend or a loved one often start
                with the word *querido(a).* Formal letters, such as business
                letters, usually start with the word *estimado(a)*
                (esteemed), instead of *querido(a),* and are followed by the
                name of the person being addressed. In English, however,
                we don't make this distinction, as we often use the term
                "dear" for both informal letters to a friend as well as
                business letters.

Viejo(a)   **Old man, Old lady**

This is the Spanish version of "old man" or "old lady." Old or not, this is what husbands and wives sometimes call one another. It is actually debatable whether or not these are terms of endearment, as some people are offended while others could care less when someone addresses them with *viejo* or *vieja*. Though it is not as common, children sometimes jokingly refer to a parent as *mi viejo* or *mi vieja*, just as we sometimes hear in the United States. Keep in mind, however, that these terms can be interpreted as disrespectful and that is why I say children say them jokingly about their parents. *No puedo quedarme tan tarde porque mi vieja me está esperando en casa* = I can't stay too late because my old lady is waiting for me at home.

9

One-Liners

Everyday Expressions, Wisecracks, Comebacks, & Snappy Answers

Nothing can say so much in so few words as a one-liner. You couldn't last even a few minutes in a conversation with native speakers without hearing some of them pop up. Other one-liners may be reserved only for certain situations. Learn these expressions well enough so that they can just roll off your tongue at that perfect moment. Timing is everything with one-liners, so don't be caught at a loss for words when you need them.

A lo hecho pecho
What's done is done

When there's no use crying over spilt milk, reminding people of this phrase may do some good. *A lo hecho pecho* means "What's done is done." You've just turned in your final exam only to realize that you answered one of the questions incorrectly. You panic desperately, but since the professor already has your paper in his hand and there's no going back, your friend sympathetically tells you, "*A lo hecho pecho.*"

A otro perro con ese hueso
Tell that line to someone else

If the vacuum salesman is trying to sell you on the point that his three-thousand-dollar vacuum cleaner will pick up one hundred and fifty times more dirt than would other leading brands and will save you money in the long run, then throw this one-liner at him. *A otro perro con ese hueso* literally means "to another dog with that bone," but it is also a euphemism for the sometimes more appropriately worded "Feed that bullshit to someone else."

¡A poco!
Really!

¡A poco! is the equivalent of "Really!" or "No way!" as we say in English and is used to express astonishment or disbelief. It is pronounced with an exclamatory falling intonation tailing at the end. *¡A poco!* would be a fitting reply when someone reveals the shocker that her friend Martha just left her husband for a man half her age.

¡Aguas!
Watch out!

Shout, "*¡Aguas!*" when warning someone about the banana peel on the staircase or the low flying pigeons coming towards you and your friends.

Ahora los patos les tiran a las escopetas
Now the roles are reversed, Now the tables are turned

This is a cute little phrase literally meaning "Now the ducks are shooting at the shotguns." This is sort of a playful one-liner one would use when someone unexpectedly reverses the roles on someone else. Let's suppose that every day you're teaching your little five-year-old niece how to dance. Much to your pleasant surprise, one day she suggests a few new moves to the routine. Impressed by her precociousness, you can tell her, "*Ahora los patos les tiran a las escopetas*," which essentially means "Now look who's trying to show whom how it's done."

Al César lo que es del César y a Dios lo que es de Dios
Give credit where credit is due

In English this means "to Caesar what is Caesar's and to God what is God's." This is quite a useful phrase meaning "to give credit where credit is due." The only problem is that it is too long and by the time you finish saying it, it sounds more like an entire verse than a one-liner. Where there's a will, there's a way, and lucky for us, this one can be shortened to *Al César lo que es del César*. The rest is understood. Just so we're clear, César refers to Julius Caesar—not the boxer and not the salad (also see "Take credit for something someone else did" in chapter 5).

¡Aunque sea!
At least!

Here's another pithy phrase. It means "At least!" and it is spoken with a hint (or a ton) of sarcasm, depending on the situation. The English translation would be something like "Better than nothing," or "That's the least you can do." Your billionaire father tells you that he's going to buy you a used car for Christmas. *"¡Aunque sea!"* you might mutter sarcastically since your expectations were more along the lines of a brand new Mercedes.

Buen intento
Nice try

This comment has two faces. It can act as well-intentioned words of comfort or a "nice try but you can't fool me" type of remark when spoken suspiciously. If Héctor struck out every time at bat in the baseball game, then his father might sympathetically tell him, *"Buen intento"* as he gives him a pat on the back. If your little sister tells the babysitter that her mother always lets her stay up late and eat all the snacks she desires, the sitter can reply with a disbelieving, *"Buen intento."*

Cada quien
To each his own

"Cada quien" is the general and abbreviated way to express that all people have their own styles, tastes, preferences, and ways of doing things. I never understood why my cousin Jaime drowns everything he eats in a sea of hot sauce, but *"Cada quien,"* he reminds me. In other words, Jaime is saying, "You eat your food the way you like it and I'll eat my food the way I like it." *Cada quien* should not be confused with the saying, *"Cada quien con su cada cual"* (Birds of a feather flock together).

¿Cómo crees que estoy?
How do you think I feel?

This is a less-than-sympathetic response to someone who seemingly has less right to complain than you. After riding on your back for half an hour, your little nephew finally gets off and tells you how tired he is. *"¿Cómo crees que estoy?"* you respond as you nearly pass out from exhaustion.

Como Pedro por su casa
Make yourself at home

Sounds like a courteous remark to tell someone visiting your home, but actually it's not as hospitable as it sounds. If you really want someone to feel right at home, then say, *"Mi casa es tu casa."* Literally, this means "My home is your home," but the more familiar translation is "Make yourself at home." Like many of the one-liners, however, this one is a sarcastic phrase and it is directed at those who have already made themselves feel right at home without needing to be told to do so. Your new neighbor comes over to introduce himself, so you invite him in. He proceeds straight to the refrigerator and helps himself to your beer, then sits in your favorite chair, and kicks his feet up on your coffee table. Though you may not say it to his face, when he leaves you could tell your friends, *"¡Mi vecino entró y agarró una cerveza como Pedro por su casa!"* ("My neighbor came in and grabbed a beer as if he were right at home!").

De haberlo sabido antes
If only I had known before

The old saying "Hindsight is 20/20" comes to life with this one-liner. This is what one would say if one bought an eighty-five-dollar, nonrefundable wool sweater just one day before the seventy-five percent blow-out sale.

De seguro
For sure

De seguro is the translation for the ever popular "For sure" as we say in English. After eating a tasty meal at the seafood restaurant, the owner tells you to visit anytime. *"De seguro,"* you assure her.

De una vez
All at once, All in one shot

A handy phrase that means "all at once," but more accurately means "might as well do it all now." After buying your groceries you see a video rental store right next door to the supermarket. Since you were going to go out for a video later that night anyway, you think, *De una vez,* and rent it right then and there; now you don't have to return and get it later.

¿De veras?
Really?

This one is very similar to *¡A poco!* *¿De veras?* also means "Really?" and expresses surprise, disbelief, or astonishment, but *¡A poco!* is the more dramatic of the two and that's why I denoted it with exclamation points instead of question marks. *¿De veras?* is usually spoken a few decibel levels down from the more enthusiastic and emphatic *¡A poco!*

Debut y despedida
First and last time

After giving your coworker a ride home that took an unexpected two hours, you console yourself by saying, "*Debut y despedida.*" In English the literal translation is "debut and farewell," but in conversation it is like saying, "That's the first and last time that'll ever happen."

Del dicho al hecho, hay mucho trecho
Easier said than done

This is a classic response for those who just make things sound so easy when the reality is quite the opposite. Suppose little Michael tells his mom that he's going to practice every day so that one day he can become a professional basketball player. Knowing that the odds are against him, she says, "*Del dicho al hecho hay mucho trecho*" ("Easier said than done"). Literally, this phrase translates to "There's a long stretch from what is said to what is done."

El pez, por su propia boca, muere
Burned by one's own big mouth

Actually, this is more of a proverb but it's also a good one-liner. Literally, it means "The fish dies by its own mouth." One can say this about people who get burned by opening their own big mouths. Though she knew better, Sally made public some private "insider" information about her company's stock forecast, which eventually got her fired. "*El pez, por su propia boca, muere,*" her coworkers commented as they watched her clean out her desk.

Él que ríe al/de último ríe mejor
He who laughs last laughs best

Being on the short end of the stick is never easy, but getting the last laugh certainly eases the pain. *Él que ríe al/de último ríe mejor* (He who laughs last laughs best) is how we express this in Spanish. Here's an example. There was one ice cream bar left in the store freezer, and as I reached for it, another customer came out of nowhere and beat me to it. Just to rub it in my face, he smirked at me while licking his ice cream bar ever so slowly. Then, as if his gloating were frowned upon by a higher source, the ice cream suddenly slipped off the stick and splattered to the ground. *"Él que ríe al/de último ríe mejor,"* I snickered to myself. Notice that this entry in Spanish gives the option of using the prepositions *al* or *de* (shown as *al/de*). The reason that I present you with both choices is because you may hear this phrase spoken with either preposition depending on the country. Spanish speakers from Mexico will use *al*, whereas Spanish speakers from other Latin American countries will use *de*.

Eso es lo de menos
That's the least of one's problems, That's the last thing on one's mind

Reserved for days when things just don't seem to be going your way, *Eso es lo de menos* is how you say, "That's the least of my worries" or "That's the last thing on my mind." You're speeding down Highway 1, already one hour late in picking up your kids, when your car breaks down. Then you remember you left the oven on with the pot roast probably burning inside by this point. After all that has happened to you, your husband says, "We have to decide what we're gonna watch on television tonight." That's your cue to say, *"Eso es lo de menos,"* since that's probably the last thing on your mind.

Eso está por verse
That remains to be seen

This phrase can be used as a challenge as if to say, "Prove it." Your lazy husband tells you that he'll clean the whole house. You can respond with, *"Eso está por verse"* ("That remains to be seen"). It's a good phrase to have handy when you need to use a little reverse psychology to challenge someone into actually doing what you need him or her to do.

Estamos a mano
We're even

Here's one that we all take great satisfaction in saying simply because it usually involves a little payback or retribution. Your big brother hits you on the arm and so you hit him back and say, "We're even" except since we're learning Spanish here, you say, *"Estamos a mano"* instead.

Esto y lo otro
This and that

In English, when someone asks you, "What have you been doing these days?" we might lazily respond, "Oh, you know ... this and that," because sometimes we just don't feel like getting into specifics. The equivalent response in Spanish would be *Esto y lo otro*.

Hogar, dulce hogar
Home sweet home

Dorothy from *The Wizard of Oz* said it best: "There's no place like home." *Hogar, dulce hogar* essentially means the same thing. After a long, tiring day at work we often breathe a sigh of relief and say, *"Hogar, dulce hogar"* as soon as we step through the front door of the house.

¡Justo a tiempo!
Just in time!   Just in the nick of time!   Perfect timing!

Use this one-liner the same way you would in English. For example, you're sitting at a café waiting for your girlfriend to arrive. Before she gets there this guy sitting next to you starts blabbering to you about something in which you have no interest. Just as you're about to lose your patience with his nonstop chattering, your girlfriend steps through door and rescues you. *"¡Justo a tiempo!"* you whisper in her ear with a sigh of relief.

Lo que no me mata me fortelece
What doesn't kill me only makes me stronger

Generally speaking, this is true, but don't take it out of context. Just because you wake up the next morning after taking way too many shots of tequila the night before doesn't mean that you're a stronger person for surviving.

Los resultados hablan por si solos
The results speak for themselves

Sure, it's a cocky response, but if you say it, it usually means that you can back it up. You know your friend Juan has been working out at the gym. The next time you see him you ask, "Have all those hours at the gym been paying off?" Juan responds, *"Los resultados hablan por si solos"* as he tears off his shirt to debut his newly sculptured abs and chiseled chest.

¡Maldito sea!
Damn it!   Damn!

¡Maldito sea! means "Damn it!" or "Damn!" It is not uncommon to hear someone say it in English, but it isn't used so frequently in everyday Spanish conversation. You will actually hear it more often in Spanish-language soap operas called *telenovelas*. So, what do people actually say instead of *¡Maldito sea!* in real conversation? You will often hear *¡Qué mala onda!* or even *¡Puta!*

Más vale prevenir que lamentar
Better (to be) safe than sorry

There are some risks that are just not worth taking, and nothing says it better than *"Más vale prevenir que lamentar"* ("Better to be safe than sorry"). Refraining from eating the three-headed fish caught near the industrial-waste plantation is a good example of this.

Más vale tarde que nunca
Better late than never

Needless to say, the proverbial "Better late than never" doesn't apply if the fire truck arrives three hours after the raging inferno burned the neighborhood to the ground. In most cases, however, this phrase does give us a little consolation as in the example of missing an important deadline. Mateo forgot his girlfriend's birthday, but the day after, he gave her flowers and said, *"Más vale tarde que nunca"* ("Better late than never"), though I doubt she would agree.

Me suena bien
Sounds good to me

"Sí," means "Yes," and we say this all the time. When asked if you want to eat tacos, see a movie, or drive around the city, you can respond, *"Sí"* if your answer is "Yes." Of course this is a perfectly good and common response, but every now and then try adding a little more enthusiasm and variation to your reply by saying, *"Me suena bien."* This phrase translates to "Sounds good to me," and though it is less frequently heard, it is a more impressive, fluent-sounding phrase. *"Sí, me late"* is another good alternative. This phrase comes from the verb *latir,* which means "to beat" (like a heart). Essentially, this expression means that eating tacos, seeing a movie, and driving around the city are all good ideas that get you up and going like the beat of your heart. Lastly, *"Sale"* is a popular phrase, often heard in Mexico, and it means the same thing. Your friend asks, *"Vamos a la película. ¿Sale?"* ("Let's go to the movies. Sound good?") *"Sale,"* you reply back.

Menos mal
Good thing

We say it all the time in English and native Spanish speakers say it all the time in Spanish. In other words, you should definitely learn this one. So, what do you say after passing the Bar exam? One good option would be, *"Menos mal porque ya no tengo que tomarlo de nuevo"* ("Good thing because now I won't have to take it again"). What do you say after finally finishing that important report for the boss just before the absolute deadline? You could say, *"Menos mal que terminé a tiempo"* ("Good thing I finished on time").

¡Mira quién habla!
Look who's talking!

The equivalent of our "Look who's talking!" After telling your little brother that he shouldn't get into fights with everyone at school, he shouts back, "*¡Mira quién habla!*" ("Look who's talking!") as he points to your black eye and toothless mouth.

Ni huele ni hiede como la mierda de gavilán
He, she, or it doesn't contribute anything to the cause

This saying is for the more daring. It's a phrase pointed at those who don't seem to have anything to offer to the conversation or don't have anything to contribute to the cause. They're just sort of sitting there like a potted plant or wallflower, similar to the guy at the party who doesn't talk, drink, or dance. The origin of this phrase comes from a type of bird called a *gavilán* (sparrowhawk), whose excrement (*mierda*) neither smells nor stinks (though I have not personally verified the validity of this claim). If you're not feeling brave enough to say it, feel free to use *ni pinta ni da color* (He or she neither paints nor gives color), which means the same thing.

¡Ni lo mande Dios!
Perish the thought!   Not even if ordered by God!

This is a great phrase. More literally it translates to "Not even if ordered by God!" Curiously enough, this phrase can be one of either hope or hopelessness, depending of course on the context in which it is spoken. For example, it is a good no-nonsense reply to that creepy scumbag who asks you out on a date because this phrase will dash any hope he may have. In this example, it is sort of like saying, "Not in a million years!" Now let's say your friend Ricardo is getting ready to have major surgery and his mother says, "*Espero que nada malo pase*" ("I hope nothing bad happens"). You can reply, "*¡Ni lo mande Dios!*" In this example, it means something more along the lines of "God would never allow it to happen!"

¡Ni lo pienses!
Don't even think about it!   Don't go there!

You're just about to finish your term paper on your computer after ten hours of grueling research. Before you have the opportunity to save all your final changes, your little brother puts his hand on the computer plug and threatens to pull it. "*¡Ni lo pienses!*" ("Don't even think about it!"), you tell him with eyes ready to pop out.

Ni modo
Oh, well

This is one of the perennial all-stars as far as one-liners go. *Ni modo* means "Oh, well" or "What can you do?" It is often spoken with a sigh of resignation or acceptance of a situation that may be beyond one's control. In fact, it almost has a "shit happens, so deal with it" connotation to it. You just got off the bus and realized that you left your lunch on the seat. "*Ni modo,*" you say to yourself, knowing that you can always buy another lunch. If you left your kid on the bus, then *Ni modo* is obviously not the appropriate response. It is typically said for things and situations you have to accept.

¡No cantas mal las rancheras!
You're not so great yourself!   You shouldn't talk!

It is a humorous replacement for *¡Mira quién habla!* (Look who's talking!). After three straight hours of playing basketball with your friends, one of your friends catches wind of your odor and shouts, "*¡Hueles feo!*" ("You stink!"). You fire back with a "*¡Tú no cantas mal las rancheras!*" ("You shouldn't talk!" or "You're not so great yourself!").

¡No hay pero que valga!
There's no buts about it!

This is what you say when you absolutely need to have a situation a certain way and it's not negotiable. When Mom says, "*¡Vas a limpiar tu cuarto y no hay pero que valga!*" ("You're going to clean your room and there's no buts about it"), that means the only "butt" is the one she'll kick (yours)—if your room is not cleaned.

No más habla, pero no actúa
All talk, no action

It's January 1ˢᵗ and, true to tradition, we make our yearly resolution: "This year I'm going to start fresh by exercising, eating right, and quitting smoking. This is the year I'm going to get my life back on track." For the few that actually follow through—congratulations! For the remainder of us, I say, *"No más habla, pero no actúa"* ("All talk, no action").

No más preguntando
Just wondering

No más preguntando = Just wondering, but you can shorten it to the simpler *No más* in which case "Just because" becomes the better translation. This simple but necessary one-liner is the perfect response to give when someone asks, "Why?" and you just don't feel like explaining. So, when someone asks, *"¿Por qué quieres saber?"* ("Why do you want to know?"), you can reply, *"No más preguntando"* ("Just wondering") or *"No más"* ("Just because").

No más ven burro y se les antoja viaje
Take advantage of a free ride

All you did was tell your friends that you're going on a weekend trip to Mexico and suddenly you're in charge of bringing something back for everyone—panchos, sombreros, T-shirts, piggy banks, you name it. It's not that anyone really needs or wants anything. Just the fact that you're going is enough for them to take advantage of the opportunity and ask for something. *No más ven burro y se les antoja viaje* is the applicable phrase in this scenario. This saying means "They just see a donkey and suddenly they feel the need to get a free trip." You may also hear the Americanismo *raite* (ride) used instead of *viaje*.

¿No qué no?
Told you so

¿No qué no? means "I told you so." It's the snappy, in-your-face way to say, *"Te dije"* ("I told you"). You tried unsuccessfully to convince your friend that it was going to rain in the evening. Sure enough, at sundown, drops, then buckets, begin to fall from the sky, drenching your friend and ruining his finely coiffed hairdo. *"¿No qué no?"* you boast from the safety of your umbrella.

No tengo ni la menor idea
I don't have the slightest idea

Has someone ever asked you for your opinion about something you have absolutely no clue about? Well, the next time this happens you can say, "*No tengo ni la menor idea*" to accompany the blank look in your eyes.

¡N'ombre!
No way!

This one is so common that you'll learn it without even trying. *¡N'ombre!* is the fusion of *no + hombre* and it means "Yeah, right!" or "Not even!" or "Get out of here!" or "No way!" It is spoken defiantly or in disbelief, but the tone in which it is said depends on the situation. Check out the following examples:

Scenario:	Your wife just informed you that she hit the big lottery jackpot.
Reply:	*¡N'ombre!* (As if to say, "Get out of here!" in a tone of disbelief).
Scenario:	Your friend asks if you want to run a fifty-six-mile marathon with him.
Reply:	*¡N'ombre!* (As if to say, "You must be crazy!").

Ojo por ojo, diente por diente
An eye for an eye, a tooth for a tooth

Like *estamos a mano* (We're even), this phrase also gives us a sense of satisfaction because it involves a little payback or retribution. You don't have to say the entire phrase. *Ojo por ojo* will suffice and you'll be understood. Alex refused to lend you twenty dollars when you desperately needed it. As karma would have it, the following week he turned to you for help when he waited in line for eight hours for concert tickets only to reach the ticket booth and find that he was short of money. "*Ojo por ojo,*" you tell him unsympathetically as you walk away with your tickets.

Ojos que no ven, corazón que no siente
Out of sight, out of mind

This phrase is a reminder of how quickly we forget, and it can be your greatest ally or your worst fear. After getting dumped by your boyfriend, a good friend might keep you and your mind as far away from him (and any reminder of him) as possible based on the theory *Ojos que no ven, corazón que no siente*. The more exact translation is "The heart doesn't feel what the eyes don't see," but it is the equivalent of our "Out of sight, out of mind." Unfortunately, this phrase can also work against you just as easily. You and your buddies are a very tightly knit and inseparable group. That is, until you move away. Suddenly your phone stops ringing, the knocking on your door ceases, and you are all but a forgotten relic from the past. *"Ojos que no ven, corazón que no siente,"* you reluctantly admit.

Pan comido
It's a cinch, It's a piece of cake

This is a confident and sometimes cocky one-liner meaning "It's a cinch," "As good as done," or "Piece of cake." Your coworker crumples up a sheet of paper into a ball and shoots it straight into the wastebasket across the room, then turns to you and says, *"Te apuesto que no puedes hacer eso"* ("Bet you can't do that"). *"Pan comido,"* you respond as you crumple another sheet of paper with a confident smirk.

Por si acaso
Just in case

For those who always like to be prepared, this one-liner will serve you well. "Why are you bringing a jacket when it's ninety-nine degrees outside?" *"Por si acaso hace frío en la noche,"* you reply ("Just in case it gets cold at night").

¡Qué agallas!
What nerve!

This is the kind of expression you would say to a wedding guest who walks over to the cake and helps himself or herself to two slices before the ceremonial first cut by the bride and groom. Then, you would tell the person, *"¡Qué agallas!"* ("What nerve!").

¿Qué esperas?
What do you expect?

You and all your roommates are moving out of one apartment and into another, but you're the only one working your tail off loading things into the truck while everyone else is standing around watching. Finally, one of the roommates asks if you need help. *"¿Qué esperas?"* you reply a little annoyed and upset. In not so many words, you're saying, "What do you expect … I'm gonna do it all by myself?"

¡Qué gacho!
What a bummer!   That sucks!

¡Qué gacho! means "That sucks!" or "What a bummer!" After your friend tells you he just got fired from his job, you might respond sympathetically, *"¡Qué gacho!"* Say this among your more informal inner circle, but when you're in unfamiliar or formal company, say, *"¡Qué malo!"* which is more appropriate.

¿Qué le hace?   ¿Qué tiene?
What's the big deal?

Not heard everywhere in the Spanish-speaking world, these phrases are a dime a dozen, at least in Mexico. Both mean the same thing, but for the sake of simplicity I will use *¿Qué le hace?* in the following example. *¿Qué le hace?* spoken as a question means "Is it okay?" or "No big deal, right?" *¿Qué le hace si me comí todas tus galletas?* = Is it okay that I ate all of your cookies? You can also attach *¿Qué le hace?* at the end of this same sentence, and it means the same thing: *Me comí todas tus galletas. ¿Qué le hace?* Actually, you're not exactly asking if it's okay. You're assuming or hoping it is, but you just want to hear the answer for yourself. Spoken as statements rather than questions, *"Qué le hace" "Qué tiene"* and *"No le hace"* are all good stand-alone replies in themselves, meaning "It's okay" or "No big deal." Note that the verbs *"hacer"* and *"tener"* are always conjugated in the third-person singular, and *"hacer"* goes with the indirect object pronoun *"le."* So, if a friend says, "Sorry I ate all of your cookies," you can respond, *"Qué le hace"* or *"Qué tiene"* or *"No le hace"* meaning "So what" or "No big deal"

¡Qué milagro!
What a miracle!

¡Qué milagro! is simply "What a miracle!" If you believe in miracles, then just have this phrase handy for that incredible day when your stingy friend finally offers to treat everyone for lunch, for example.

¡Qué padre!
How cool!   How awesome!

In Mexico, many colloquial expressions and slang terms associated with the word *padre* (father) describe things that are totally cool or awesome. The most widely used of all such expressions is *¡Qué padre!* (How cool! or How awesome!) Respond with *"¡Qué padre!"* after your friend shows you his sleek, new car or after taking a tour of his beautifully remodeled home, for example. *¡Qué padre!* is a very Mexican expression, but it is widely understood among non-Mexican Spanish speakers in the United States.

¡Qué poco te duró el chiste!
Your victory didn't last!

This is the comeback response to someone whose victory didn't last long enough to be enjoyed. Your classmate is gloating over the fact that he beat you in the semifinals of your school sit-ups competition. He will advance to the finals but has suddenly developed a severe case of diarrhea, and his participation could have seriously embarrassing consequences. *"¡Qué poco te duró el chiste!"* you tell him ("Your victory didn't last long!").

¡Qué raquítico!
How skimpy!

¡Qué raquítico! generally means "How skimpy!" One might be tempted to say this after lifting the top bun off one's burger only to find a hamburger patty fit for a Barbie doll. *¡Qué raquítico(a)!* in this scenario means "What skimpy portions!" Don't let the waiter or chef hear you because it's not exactly the smartest or most polite thing you could say especially if you have more entrees coming out. This one-liner can also be said about the eighty-pound supermodel or even about the skimpy bikini she's wearing.

¿Quién manda?
Who gives the orders?

¿Quién manda? = "Who gives the orders?" or "Who's the boss?" Regina and her husband are having a little argument in front of you. Jokingly, you say, *"A ver, quién manda"* for "Let's see who's the boss." Here's another example. Suppose your friend visits you at work and starts telling your employees what to do. *"¿Quién manda?"* you ask him as you reestablish your authority. Though literally you asked, "Who gives the orders?" the message you're communicating is more like, "Look, I'm the boss around here and I give the orders." The younger folk have another more hip and colloquial option if they so choose—*Aquí no más mis chicharrones truenan* (Here, I give the orders). Literally, it means "Here only my pork skins crackle." It's practically a tongue-twister. Try saying this without tripping over your words and you'll soon realize why *¿Quién manda?* might suit you better.

¿Quién te manda?
Serves you right, You asked for it

This is a somewhat unsympathetic expression to tell someone who should have known better. This entry sounds very similar to the previous one (*¿Quién manda?*), but it is quite different in meaning. *¿Quién te manda?* literally asks, "Who ordered you?" but in conversation, it is translated more like the statement "Serves you right" or "You asked for it." For example, suppose you went to visit your cousin Daniel, who is always rude and snobby to you. After you get home you begin complaining to your friends how Daniel was once again his rude and snobby self. Well, since his bad attitude never surprises anyone and everybody knows he won't change, your friends reply, *"¿Quién te manda?"* Essentially, your friends are saying, "Well, nobody forced you to go."

Sano y salvo
Safe and sound

Like *Hogar, dulce hogar* (home sweet home), we might say, *"Sano y salvo"* with a sigh of relief when arriving safely back to the house after driving three hours in a heavy thunderstorm.

¡*Tal para cual!*
Two of a kind!

It can be used as sort of a wisecrack or teasing comment people might snicker to each other when a father and son dressed exactly alike walk into the room, for example.

The Verbs *Ser* and *Querer*

Used to express: Whatever, whenever, whoever, wherever, however

Note: Before you begin reading the next part, I must tell you that this section will become an indispensable part of your everyday conversations in Spanish. I'm not asking you to learn this section; I'm demanding it.

Someone asks what you want to eat for dinner and you respond with an accommodating, "Whatever," or "Whatever you want." A friend asks where you want to go this weekend. You say, "Wherever," or "Wherever you want." Someone asks how to prepare your steak. "However," or "However you want," you respond. Another asks what time you want to go. "Whenever," or "Whenever you want," you answer. We use these flexible, go-with-the-flow responses all the time. The verbs *ser* (to be) and *querer* (to want) make it possible for us to do the same in Spanish. Both require the use of the subjunctive. From *ser* we get some wide-open, general responses: *lo que sea* (whatever), *cuando sea* (whenever), *donde sea* (wherever), *quien sea* (whoever), and *como sea* (however). This *sea* construction (pronounced *seh-ah*) will never change, so you don't need to conjugate the verb.

Querer gives us an equally valuable one-liner but requires a little more attention to detail. Like *sea*, you will attach the subjunctive form of the verb (in this case, *querer*) after *lo que* (what), *cuando* (when), *donde* (where), *quien* (who), or *como* (how). Unlike the unchanging *sea*, however, you will be required to conjugate the verb *querer* in the subjunctive form according to who is being addressed in the sentence.

Now here's the important part. What in the heck do these one-liners mean? Pay very close attention to the examples to follow, and the picture should start to come into focus. Each example contains a question. The first reply is derived from *ser,* and the second reply is derived from *querer.*

Expressing "Whatever"

Question: *¿Qué les damos de comer?*
                (What should we feed them?)

Reply: *Lo que sea.* (Whatever.)

Reply: *Lo que quieran.* (Whatever they want.)

Expressing "Whenever"

Question: *¿Cuándo quieres ir?* (When do you want
                to go?)

Reply: *Cuando sea.* (Whenever.)

Reply: *Cuando quieras.* (Whenever you want.)

Expressing "Wherever"

Question: *¿Dónde nos podemos encontrar?* (Where
                can we meet?) (formal)

Reply: *Donde sea.* (Wherever.)

Reply: *Donde quiera usted.* (Wherever you want.)

Expressing "Whoever"

Question: *¿A quién invitará Pedro a la fiesta?* (Who
                should Pedro invite to the party?)

Reply: *A quien sea.* (Whoever.)

Reply: *A quien quiera.* (Whoever he wants.)

Expressing "However"

Question: *¿Cómo planeamos nuestro viaje?* (How
                shall we plan our trip?)

Reply: *Como sea.* (However.)

Reply: *Como queramos.* (However we want.)

Trato hecho
It's a deal

It's what we say to seal bets, promises, agreements, and negotiations. After bargaining back and forth with the vendor at the souvenir shop, you finally hear a price to which you can agree. So, before the vendor has a chance to change her mind, you say, *"Trato hecho"* ("It's a deal") as you hand her the money and walk away, happy.

¿Tú, qué sabes?
What do you know?

We can challenge people's knowledge and opinions with this one. It means "What do *you* know?" and it is often spoken with a contentious tone. For example, if your mother tries to tell you how to raise your kids when she herself was never there for her own kids, then you can use this one-liner on her.

¡Una cucharada de tu propia medicina!
A taste of your own medicine!

A good phrase for someone who just had it coming. The English equivalent would be "A taste of your own medicine!" Just as it is in the hierarchy of the food chain, Big Bully Butch picked on all the smaller kids in his class. Ten years and two hundred pounds later, Bully Buster Bob (previously known as "Little Bob," and former human punching bag for Butch) gave Butch *una cucharada de su propia medicina* and put him in his place.

¡Vamos de nuevo!
Here we go again!

When history repeats itself, we can whip this one out with a frustrated sigh and our hands thrown up in the air. *"¡Vamos de nuevo!"* is what you might say when the weekend rolls around and like clockwork you're rudely awakened in the wee hours of Sunday morning by the wild party-goers blasting music from their cars.

Y por si fuera poco
And if that weren't enough

When an already unbelievable story gets even better (or worse), we often say, "And if that weren't enough … " as we continue to explain the unbelievable events that unfolded. Christian had everyone's sympathy as he explained to his friends how a robber stole all of his jewelry, money, and electronic equipment from his house. He then continued, "*¡Y por si fuera poco me robó mi ropa interior también!*" ("And if that weren't enough, he even stole my underwear, too!").

¡Ya chole!   ¡Ya está choteado(a)!
That's old already!

¡Ya chole! and *¡Ya está choteado(a)!* both come from the verb *chotear* (See "Get old" from chapter 5). This one-liner is the perfect response to express your weariness with worn-out jokes, radio tunes, fashion trends, or anything else that has worn out its novelty. Let's say for the sake of this example that your name is Brad. Every time you give your name to someone or make reservations at a restaurant or hotel the person you're speaking with jokingly says, "Like Brad Pitt?" as if it were the most original joke ever told. Since it's the oldest joke in the book as far as you're concerned, you could reply, "*¡Ya chole!*" or "*¡Ya está choteado!*" In this context, it translates roughly to "That one's already too old," or "I've heard that one a million times." Warning: This comeback response will likely come across as a little rude unless spoken to someone who can take a joke.

¿Ya ves?
Now you see?   See what I mean?

This is one of the more indispensable of the one-liners. It literally means "Now you see?" or "See what I mean?" and is derived from the verb *ver* (to see). It's an "I told you so" type of reply that emphasizes that you just knew something was going to happen … and it did. In spite of many warnings from his parents, Tomás continued to rock back and forth in his chair at the dinner table until one day he couldn't keep his balance and fell back, crashing onto the floor. "*¿Ya ves?*" his parents yell as they wave their fingers at him.

10

No Man's Land

Useful Vocabulary
That Didn't Make the Cut

Like a dollar bill tossed away by the wind and landing in a deserted field, the phrases provided in this section do have practical value—they just didn't find their way into any of the previous chapters. So here they have congregated to form their own section in what I have dubbed "No Man's Land." I can almost guarantee you that, like karma, every word you hear will come back to you down the road, so don't take anything for granted. The words contained in this section are a collection of tricky homonyms, false cognates, hybrid phrases, and other odds and ends that I gleaned from my daily wanderings through the streets of Mexico. I hope you find them useful. Better yet, why not start your own list?

A domicilio   **Home delivery**

Don't feel like getting off the couch and driving out for a bite to eat? Just call a restaurant that offers *A domicilio* and have the food delivered right to your door instead.

A la medida   **Perfect fit**

A la medida refers to things, not people. For example, you don't say, "*a la medida*" for a couple that looks good together, but you can say this about the garage cabinets you built that fit perfectly to the last inch.

A medias   **Half-assed**

One of the main reasons why lazy people often have to work double is because they do things *a medias*. That is, they do things half-assed.

Aduanas   **Customs**

Aduanas means "customs," but it has nothing to do with culture and traditions. We can certainly, however, learn about the cultures and traditions of other countries after getting our passports stamped by *aduanas* upon arrival in the airport during our vacation abroad.

Ahorcapollos   **Flip-flops, Thongs**

Ahorcapollos is more of a Mexican term for this casual footwear for walking on the beach and around the swimming pool. However, since this is a very regional term, be ready to use *chanclas* or *chancletas* as other options.

Amor apache   **Love-hate**

Yes, love can certainly be a painful experience but even more so when the kind of relationship you have is *amor apache*.

Anticipo   **Advance (payment)**

An *anticipo* is an advance payment one makes to reserve something, such as a clubhouse or ballroom for a party.

Arroz, Arroz frito, y Morisqueta   **Rice**

Arroz is rice but you already knew that. Did you know that fried rice is *arroz frito* and that steamed white rice is *morisqueta*? Now you do.

Banqueta   **Sidewalk**

Banqueta means "sidewalk," not "banquet." A banquet (like the kind you go to for an awards ceremony) is a *banquete*.

Barrida   Sweep

Usually a term heard in the sports world, a *barrida* is a "sweep." If the Dodgers beat the Yankees four times in a row to win the World Series, then that would be a *barrida*.

Bienestar   Well-being

You may not actually use this word all that often, but you should always keep your own *bienestar* in mind when it comes to your health.

Borrón y cuenta nueva   Clean slate

This is a popular phrase for those who need to start fresh after a bad breakup. *Borrón* means "blot" or "smudge," and in this phrase, it refers to blotting out or erasing. *Cuenta nueva* means "new count," so this expression means "erasing and counting over." You may recognize this phrase as the more familiar "clean slate" or "turning over a new leaf."

Cabezear   Nod off

Cabeza means "head." So it makes sense that *cabezear* is the verb for "nodding off" like when you're falling asleep in class or in the car and your head slowly starts to bob up and down.

Carnada   Bait

Worms, jiggers, and squid are often used as *carnada* to catch fish, but you can also use candy as *carnada* to bait your little brother.

Carne deshebrada   Shredded beef

A definite must-know for those who like their enchiladas, burritos, chimichangas, and other dishes with shredded beef. *Carne desmenusada* is another term for shredded beef.

Carpeta   File folder, Binder

Don't forget that a *carpeta* in Spanish is not a "carpet" in English. A *carpeta* is actually a file folder or binder. "Carpet," like the type we might place over a wooden floor, is *alfombra* in Spanish.

Cartas, Barajas, y Tarjetas   Cards

Cartas are actually letters, as in written letters. Playing cards are *barajas* or *cartas*. Greeting cards, credit cards, phone cards, and business cards are *tarjetas*. Business cards, however, can also be called *tarjetas de negocios*.

Chapopote   Asphalt

I learned this one because my in-laws live on the edge of a bustling intersection in Mexico and they are constantly sweeping the *chapopote* brought in from the street. The general and more universal word for asphalt is *asfalto*.

Cheque vs. Cuenta   Check

Both mean "check," but *cuenta* refers to the one you ask the waiter for after your meal and *cheque* refers to the one you write out to pay your bills.

Chistes, Puntadas, y Bromas   Jokes

All three terms mean the same thing. Hint: You should have some handy. Having a good sense of humor is a great way to create good conversation and build relationships with native speakers.

Comezón, Picazón   Itch

These are the general terms for an itch. Keep in mind that both terms take the feminine article *la*. Also, skip ahead to *piquete* in this chapter.

Comida chatarra   Junk food

Chips, donuts, candy, cakes, and fries are some of the many devilishly tempting foods that fall into the category called *comida chatarra*.

Criminal   Criminal

A criminal is someone who has committed wrongdoing, but to say that something is *criminal* means "totally cool" or "awesome," and it's probably because something that cool could not possibly be legal.

Dados   Dice
These are the little cubes that determine our fate at the craps table.

De adorno   For decoration
Lights and ornaments on a Christmas tree and memorabilia adorning the walls of a restaurant are "for decoration" or *de adorno.*

Desempate   Tiebreaker
The best of seven series is tied three games apiece. The seventh and deciding game would be the *desempate.*

Día festivo   Holiday
Since we so relish our holidays, might as well know this one.

Diarrea, Chorro   Diarrhea
Many a gringo in Mexico has fallen victim to this gastrointestinal volcanic reaction when eating too much chile or drinking unpurified water.

Embarazada   Pregnant
A classic and comical blunder that could cost you a good dose of humiliation. When you're embarrassed, say, *"Me da vergüenza"* or *"Me da pena."* If you say, *"Estoy embarazada"* instead, then you've just said, "I'm pregnant."

Entre semana   Weekday
Why do we complain how fast time flies when so many of us want these five days to pass quickly only to enjoy the next two?

Escenario vs. Etapa   Stage
A physical stage for performers is *escenario.* A stage in someone's life is *etapa.*

Estira y afloja   **Give and take**

This is the key phrase for any successful relationship.

Etiqueta   **Label**

Though it sounds similar to the English word "etiquette," the word *etiqueta* has nothing to do with manners. For that, *educación* is the correct word. Examples of *etiquetas* are price tags or care labels sewn inside of your clothes.

Excitado(a)   **Horny**

Excitado(a) in Spanish means "horny" or sexually aroused, but your first inclination may be to use it for "excited" like when you're excited about the new action movie coming out, for example. When you're excited (but not horny), then use *emocionado(a)*.

Éxito   **Success**

Éxito means "success," not "exit." If you're in a Spanish-speaking country and you're looking for the nearest exit out of the theater, then look for the *salida*.

Fábrica   **Factory**

Denim, linen, polyester, and corduroy are not types of *fábricas,* but they could very well have been manufactured in one. The word for "fabric" is *tela*.

Fecha de vencimiento   **Expiration date**

Always a good idea to check this before buying your milk.

Fin de semana   **Weekend**

For those who work Monday through Friday, this is what we live for.

Fritanga   **Fried food**

French fries, onion rings, and fried chicken all fall under the category of *fritanga*.

Hechizo vs. *Encanto*   **Spell**

The ill-willed spell that turned the prince into a frog is an *hechizo*. The magical spell that made the princess fall in love with the new prince (and former frog) is an *encanto*. After your honeymoon is over, some might jokingly tell you, "*Se te acabó el encanto*" ("The magic has ended").

Hilo dental   **Floss**

Hilo dental is dental floss, but bikinis are also sometimes referred to as *hilo dental.*

Historietas   **Comics**

Historietas is the correct term for comic books and comic strips. *Cómicos* are comedians. By the way, reading *historietas en español* is an excellent way to learn Spanish.

Impuesto   **Duty, Tax**

If required, importers must pay this when bringing merchandise into the country.

Infarto   **Heart attack**

Infarto sounds more like a gastrointestinal reaction to a large meal, but it does in fact mean "heart attack."

Intimidades   **Personal things**

Love letters and cherished secrets are all some of the personal things we call *intimidades.*

Iva   **Tax**

They say that this is one thing in life we can be sure of (besides death).

La neta   **Plain truth**

When someone asks for *la neta*, he or she wants the straight, bottom-line truth. *La neta* refers to the "net truth" after all the superfluous details have been weeded out.

La vida cotidiana   **Daily life**

It's kind of the whole point of this book—to expose you to the daily-life conversations of a native Spanish speaker.

Marca patito   **Generic brand**

For those nonlabel lovers who would rather pay a lower price for things that are *marca patito*, more power to you. Notice how *marca* ends with a feminine "*a*" and *patito* ends with the masculine "*o*." So, which article, *la* or *el*, does it take? The answer is neither. The word *marca patito* does not need an article. *No me importa que la ropa sea marca patito, mientras sea de buena calidad* = I don't care that the clothes are a generic brand as long as they're good quality.

Marqueta   **Block**

Marqueta is the word for "block" as in a block of frozen shrimp, for example. It does not mean "market," though you may often hear it spoken incorrectly as such (but spelled "marketa"). The correct word for market is *mercado*.

Mascota   **Pet**

If you thought that the Spanish word *mascota* would translate to the English word "mascot," you would be right, but it's even more important to remember that its primary usage is "pet."

Matriz   **Headquarters**

This word is feminine *(la matriz)*. You can also say *oficina central* for "headquarters." While we're on the subject, *sucursal* is the word for "branch office."

Medidas avanzadas   **Drastic measures**

When all else fails, it's time to take *medidas avanzadas*.

Mosca, Cierre, y Bragueta   Fly

The annoying fly buzzing around your food is a *mosca*. Both *cierre* and *bragueta* refer to the "fly" of your pants. *Cierre* is the actual zipper (but can refer to any zipper, not just the one on your pants). *La bragueta* is the strip of fabric covering the pant zipper.

Mosquitero vs. Pantalla   Screen

The screen door that lets the air in and keeps the mosquitos out is called a *mosquitero* (but don't forget that the word for "mosquito" is *zancudo*). Television screens, movie screens, and the like are called *pantallas*.

¿Para aquí o para llevar?   For here or to go?

Often the first thing the cashier at a fast-food restaurant will ask after you place your order. If eating in the restaurant, you can respond by saying, "*Para aquí.*" If you'd rather take it to go, then say, "*Para llevar.*"

Pecados   Sins

May he who is without these cast the first stone.

Piquete   Bug bite

Typically refers to mosquito bites (*los piquetes de zancudos*). The word *piquete* is arguably the more common word used in casual conversation; however, *picadura* is the more proper word. Doctors, for example, are likely to say *picadura* instead of *piquete*.

Plenitud   Prime

This term generally refers to our best or "prime" years, whether it be the prime of life (*la plenitud de la vida*) or the prime of a career (*la plenitud de la carrera*).

Pochote   Lint

This terms applies to the balled up thread one can find in one's pant pocket as well as the clumps of dust, hair, and thread one sweeps up from the kitchen floor.

Policía   Police

It may be against your company *policía* to wear shorts to work, but that's if your company employs fashion police, because *policía* means "police," not policy. For "company policy," you will hear *reglas de la empresa* or *reglamento de la empresa.*

Pulpa   Flesh

Pulpo means octopus, but *pulpa* is not a female octopus. *Pulpa* means "pulp" like that of an orange. It also means "flesh," like the flesh of a skinned fish, but not for the flesh of beef and pork. For beef, you say, *"carne"* and for pork, *"carne de puerco."*

Quehacer   Chore

Just remember that *qué* = "what" and that *hacer* = "to do," so *los quehaceres* are your everyday "what to do's" or chores.

Racha   Streak

When you can't lose at the blackjack table, then you're on a *racha buena* (good streak). The baseball player who struck out the last ten times at the plate is on a *racha mala* (bad streak).

Receta   Prescription

Not to be confused with *recibo* (receipt), which is what you get after you make a purchase. A *receta* refers to a prescription you get from your doctor or a recipe to make your favorite dish.

Recovecos   Ins and outs

If you know the back-alley shortcuts and the hole-in-the-wall restaurants, and you can get around the city practically blindfolded, then you know the *recovecos* (ins and outs) of your city.

Recta final   Home stretch

After a long and difficult journey, this is the light at the end of the tunnel.

Rompecabezas vs. Crucigrama   Puzzle

Literally, the term *rompecabezas* means "head breaker," and refers to jigsaw puzzles and riddles. *Crucigramas* are crossword puzzles.

Ropa   Clothes

Ropa (clothes), for obvious reasons, is often confused with "rope." Don't we all wish Spanish were that easy? "Rope" is actually *cuerda, mecate*, or *soga*.

Sanalotodo   Cure-all

Sometimes it's that sweet apple pie, ice cream, or even a good joke that is the best *sanalotodo* (cure-all) when we're feeling down or sick.

Semáforo   Traffic light

It rules the streets, it tells us what to do and we obey, and it commands our attention; therefore, we should know this word, if only out of respect.

Sobras   Leftovers

A term usually reserved for leftover food, but if your ex-boyfriend Beto starts dating your own good friend *Celia* (or possible ex-friend), then you may also disdainfully tell Celia, *"Te dejo las sobras"* ("I leave you the leftovers").

Surrapas   Crumbs, Scraps

A little something you leave for the pigeons—like bread or cookie crumbs that fall off the table.

Tablas   Break-even

You use this phrase when someone asks how you did at the blackjack table and you respond by saying, *"Salí tablas."* That means that you ended up even, which is more than most people can boast.

Talla vs. Tamaño   **Size**

Talla means "size" but refers to standard sizes that can be measured, like your shoe size or the size of your pants. *Tamaño* also means "size" but is used when referring to the general physical size of something. *¿De qué tamaño es tu perro?* = What size is your dog?

Tianguis   **Flea market**

In Mexico, *tianguis* (masculine) is the better word for flea market. Outside of Mexico, however, *mercado de pulgas* (flea market) or *la pulga* are quite common.

Tope   **Speed bump**

Tope means "speed bump." It means to slow down in areas where extra caution is required. You might have run into a few of these along the way while reading this book. Literally, a *tope* is a "butt" as you may have playfully butted heads with a child. A hard, painful head butt, like in a boxing match, is called a *cabezazo*.

Traductor(a)   **Translator**

With enough practice in the Spanish language, this could be your next profession.

Tufo   **Stench**

Tufo is "stench" but when you need to verbally express how bad the stench is, say, "*¡Fuchi!*" which is like how we say, "Ewwwwh!" in English.

Zurdo(a)   **Lefty**

When nothing you do is "right," then maybe you're a "lefty" or *zurdo(a)*.

Index